Discovering Devon

A STORY OF LIFE AND SUNFLOWER

BY AMY PRICE

DEDICATION

This book is dedicated to teens everywhere.
You are not alone.

ACKNOWLEDGMENTS

I feel extraordinarily grateful to the following individuals and organizations who helped make this novel possible. First, I would like to thank my husband, Jody Price, whose support for my creative ideas has always been unfaltering. Next, I would like to thank Jim Zebora for his belief in my vision, and his careful and supportive editing, which enhanced the content and readability of this work...I could not have done this without you. Just as importantly, I would like to thank Barbara Fail, for her belief and support in my vision and her ability to take it from manuscript to a fully published work. Her artistic vision has helped make Devon a real person. I would like to thank the Eldorado Writer's Group, who listened to my rough draft, and supported my vision as it evolved. Special thanks go to all of my wonderful friends who believe in me and provide encouragement and interest for my work, especially Sandi Rusch, who eagerly read initial portions of my manuscript and begged me to write more. And thank you Steven Natanson for your enthusiasm and photography. I would also like to acknowledge Cindy Etler for her candid honesty and moving autobiography about her time with Straight, Inc. She provided me with invaluable insider information about adolescent rehabilitation programs that operated without professional oversight in the 1980s. And thank you to all the survivors of both Straight, Inc. and other RTC programs who have documented your experiences. I would also like to thank the ASTART.org and SAMHSA organizations for the important work that they do to educate and help struggling teens and their families, as well as the professionals who work with them.

CONTENTS

Title

Copyright

Dedication

Acknowledgments

Contents

PREFACE

This is a work of fiction and the product of my imagination. While it was inspired by true events, it is not meant to reflect on specific people, or specific private residential treatment centers. Any similarity is entirely coincidental. Geographical settings used are real places, but the people involved are from my imagination and do not represent actual people who live, have lived, or worked in these locations.

When I originally came up with the idea to write this novel, it was simply going to be a coming-of-age novel about a girl who was conceived at Woodstock. But, over time, the concept evolved into much more than that. I had always intended to have the main character enter an inpatient rehab facility as an adolescent because that was a common treatment for substance use in the 1980s.

During the mid to late 1980,s, I was a graduate student pursuing a doctorate in School Psychology, and had completed a literature review of adolescent substance abuse treatment for my Psy.D. project/dissertation. Much of the research available then was done on adults and the treatment protocols for adolescents were an outgrowth of that. The conventional wisdom at the time was that experimentation with a substance of any kind was considered dangerous, which often led to intensive treatment. This was the era of "just say no" to drugs and total abstinence was urged. Inpatient treatment was the first option tried in many (but not all) cases, especially because insurance companies paid for it. One of the most highly regarded programs in my area was a private inpatient hospital that was considered the gold standard of treatment. It was later sold due to insurance fraud and unnecessary admission of patients by physicians who received financial incentives. Outpatient treatment did exist, but was not always the first option tried. Follow-up care was not always provided by inpatient programs, and often consisted of recommending attendance at AA or other 12-Step programs. Most treatment models used AA/12-Step meetings as either an adjunct or significant component of treatment. Mental health professionals were advised that an adolescent needed to be sober before taking him/her as a therapy client and that the client needed to attend 12-Step meetings. Certified substance abuse counseling was a growing field and did not necessarily require graduate degrees. Many substance abuse counselors were recovering addicts who later became certified but did not have graduate-level mental health training. Although, in reputable facilities, they were supervised by those who had graduate degrees in addition to substance abuse certifications.

I am now a retired (and inactive New Jersey-licensed) School Psychologist. Treatment approaches evolved significantly over the 25 years I was in practice. There are several different therapies and treatment approaches available today which give parents and teens options. Placement in the least restrictive environment is a standard of practice, both in schools and mental health or therapeutic settings. Inpatient treatment (especially residential treatment for more than acute care) is now considered a last resort to be used after all community supports have been tried (e.g. outpatient therapy, intensive outpatient therapy, in-home family therapy, or in the case of schools, therapeutic day schools). Residential placement is made by a team of mental health profession-als, including the parent, and students are involved in their treatment plans, as well as associated agencies such as child protective services. Public schools do not place students in residential programs, but are responsible for oversight of the educational portion if they are funding the education piece and the student is registered in their district.

The majority of programs I worked with were day programs, although I did have students placed in residential programs by mental health professionals or parents.

The majority of professionals I worked with were caring and well-meaning people who genuinely wanted to improve the lives of children and adolescents. I had many positive experiences with directors and principals of day programs, the majority of which were not residential. What you will read here is not based on my personal experiences. It is not meant to be an indictment of residential mental health programs, substance abuse or other therapeutic programs. Many well-run programs use behavior modification systems, group counseling and recreational therapy. I have seen students thrive when placed in the right program for them.

However, in doing extensive research for this book, I came across documentation of cases and survivor stories where, unfortunately, that was not the case. This has been an extremely painful book for me to research and write because my favorite population to work with was oppositional adolescents. The majority of adolescents I worked with responded to having a safe, non-judgmental person to talk with, who could also provide limit setting as needed. There were times when more was needed and when a structured therapeutic setting or, sadly, incarceration was necessary. But this was usually when there was involvement with the legal system or drug abuse with narcotics, the adolescent's life was truly in danger and outpatient and community supports were not working.

What I learned in my research for this novel was that, unfortunately, that has not always been the case. Facilities have operated under secrecy with little oversight. Adolescents were being placed in locked facilities for months and sometimes years because they experimented with a substance. As noted above, it was a common belief that experimenting was equivalent to addiction and dependency, and that all adolescents minimize the extent of their use. In some situations that was true, but not all. There were cases when a determination was made with a checklist filled out by the parent and given to a non-degreed or para-professional whose only credential was that they were a recovering addict or alcoholic, or sales consultant for the program, as opposed to a licensed professional who was qualified to make a diagnosis. Abuse of children can happen in any environment where a staff member is not vetted properly, has a criminal history and managed to slip through the cracks, or is allowed to operate without supervision (in the case of para-professionals), is poorly compensated or is even misguided and unaware of potential impacts of interventions. While this is not the norm, it happens, and is more likely to happen when a program has no or poor oversight.

I am not writing this to make recommendations for treatment. Nor do I advocate alcohol or substance use by adolescents. However, I do believe that parents and adolescents should know their options and rights regarding treatment and be fully informed when selecting a program. I have included links to the following websites that have guidelines to help choose (or avoid) a program. As I mentioned above, there are many legitimate and well-regarded programs that have served many teens. However, there are also programs that look like they are reputable but have very slick marketing practices and promotional materials. Several programs that were in operation during the time frame of this novel and in the first decade of this century have been closed due to allegations of abuse, unethical financial practices and lack of appropriate accreditation.

For more information:

- ASTART

This is a non-profit advocacy group made up of professionals, parents and teens. It is a site that is designed to educate people about the private residential teen treatment industry and provides information regarding what to consider when choosing a program. It is an independent organization that does not make referrals or recommendations to specific facilities. They also provide information for parents regarding normal teen behavior and how to distinguish it from pathological or dangerous behavior.

For more information, www.astartforteens.org

• The FTC has released guidelines for residential treatment facilities for adolescents. They can be found at: consumer.ftc.gov

• If you, your teenager or someone you know is at risk for harm to self or others, especially if he or she expresses a desire to commit suicide, along with a plan to commit suicide and a way to commit suicide, please call 911. Other resources to use in a crisis:

• National Suicide Prevention Line: 1-800-273-TALK
Thoughts of suicide should always be assessed by an appropriate mental health professional immediately.

A resource for mental health and drug addiction treatment:
• SAMHSA Treatment Referral Helpline, 1-877-SAMHSA7 (1-877-726-4727). This number can be used for referrals for treatment in your local area (in the U.S.).

I would like to give special thanks and acknowledgment to Cyndy Etler, survivor of Straight Inc. and Teen Life Coach. Her books and website provide an invaluable resource and give the reader insight into how she was affected by a well-known residential treatment program in the 1980s. It is no longer in operation but offshoots have been started and still exist today. Cyndy's books are entitled *Dead Inside* and *We Can't Be Friends*.

For more information, her website is cindyetler.com

It is my hope that this novel will serve as a way to educate teens and parents about adolescent behavior and appropriate teen treatment.

-- Amy Price

PROLOGUE

Paula stood on the side of westbound Route 17A with her right arm stretched out hoisting her thumb and holding a sign that said "Woodstock" in her left hand. Clad in a suede halter top and cut-off jeans, backpack slung over her shoulder, she smiled at the oncoming traffic, hoping for a ride. The day was already promising to be a warm one and drops of sweat began to pool on her forehead near the edges of her long, strawberry blonde hair.

Just when she was beginning to lose hope, a car full of college kids from New Paltz pulled up. A guy in the front seat, with long brown hair leaned out the window and called out, "Need a ride to Woodstock?"

"Far out! Thanks!" Paula said and jumped in the back seat which held a girl about her age, with long brown hair and another guy with shoulder-length hair and a mustache.

The driver, a guy about 20, with a wild, frizzy mane, turned around and smiled, handed her a joint and said, "Hi. I'm Mark. Welcome aboard!"

And so began Paula's first journey away from her home in Warwick, New York. Paula was 18 and had just graduated from high school this past June. So far most of her summer was spent manning the farm stand that her family operated, and greeting tourists who were heading up state from the city for a day in the country. She was due to start at SUNY Binghamton as a freshman in the fall.

This was a big deal in her family. As the oldest child, Paula was the first of her generation to attend college. Warwick was a farming community and her father had one of the oldest dairy farms in the area. It was also known for its apples, and had one of the more lucrative apple orchards in the county. Generations of Paula's family had resided in Warwick, attended the United Methodist Church in town, served on the town council and were part of the Rotary Club.

When tickets for Woodstock came on sale Paula knew she

had to score one. But she couldn't tell anyone she knew she was going and had to come up with an elaborate plan. Her boyfriend Jim was already in Vietnam. He had received his induction notice before the end of the school year and had to report right after graduation. None of Paula's girlfriends wanted to make the trip to Bethel, so it was up to her to devise a plan. She told her parents that her college was having a weekend orientation in Binghamton for the freshman class to meet each other and that she would be staying in the dorm there. So far they had not suspected a thing.

It had worked and here she was riding along in a red '67 Chevy sedan, painted with peace signs and flowers in a psychedelic pattern. It held three college kids from SUNY New Paltz, smoking a J and listening to Jimi Hendrix and the Grateful Dead. Little did she know her life was about to change drastically.

1980 and 1981

March 3rd, 1980

My name is Devon Anderson. I am 9 years old. I'll be 10 soon, on May 17th. My teacher told my Gram at a parent conference that "Devon has a talent for writing and it should be encouraged." So Gram bought me this journal. She gave it to me and told me to write. I am not really sure what I'm supposed to write about, so I'll just tell about myself, I guess. I live in Warwick, New York with my Gram and Gramps on a farm just outside of town. We have cows and an apple orchard.

I have a mother but I never see her. The last time I saw her I was six months old. Gram said she ran away to live on a commune in Taos, New Mexico that was named after a pig. When I ask her about my Mom she says that she "Lost her way." If that is true, why doesn't Gram send her a map? Then she can come home. I get a birthday card from my Mom once a year. Her real name is Paula but she calls herself Sunflower. She sends a picture with each card. She is pretty and has long strawberry blonde hair (that's what Gram calls the color). But she looks like she hasn't had a bath or shower in years. Maybe that's because they worship pigs.

We worship the Lord. Gram is always talking about the Lord. As in, "If the Lord is willing, we will have a good harvest this year." We go to the United Methodist Church in town. It's one of the oldest churches in Warwick. Most of the people I know go there. I go to Sunday School while the grown-ups have church service. Our Sunday school teacher calls us her "little lambs". I guess she really meant it about me because last Christmas I was a lamb in the pageant. But I really like to sing. When I'm 12 I can be in the choir. Sometimes I make up words to songs, too. Gram wants me to learn to play piano, but I want to play guitar someday. My hands are too small now to make the chords.

I haven't said much about Gramps. He is quiet but nice.

He spends most of the day working on the farm, when I am at school and on the weekends, too. He works hard so he is tired at night. He likes to watch TV after dinner and drink beer. Except for Sunday when he goes to church with me and Gram. But, if there is a football or baseball game on he watches that and drinks beer. Gramps likes his beer. Gram does not like that. She doesn't drink, but says that a man is the King of his Castle and that wives obey their husbands. Monday is Poker Night. Gram doesn't like that because she says gambling is a sin. But Gramps said it's only penny poker. I think he just does it to get out of the house and be with other men and drink beer in peace.

Oh well, I can't think of anything else to say.

April 30th, 1981

I have been really busy at school this year so I haven't had time to write. We get a lot of homework. I am a really good student. My teacher, Miss Rumson, says I have creative ideas. I don't know about that. I do like to think a lot though. We have to write a letter of thanks to our mothers for Mother's Day. I have no idea what to write. I was thinking of asking if I could write about Gram, since I don't really feel like I have a Mom. I never see her. Sometimes I wonder if she really exists, although somebody named Sunflower sends me a birthday card every year. I don't have a father either. Gram said my Mom didn't know who he was. How is that possible? I'm old enough to know the stork did not bring me. Gram says she'll tell me about it when I'm older. But I know more than she thinks. I listen when people talk and I found out some information. Sunflower used to be a normal kid who was a cheerleader and in the yearbook club. She had a boyfriend in high school who got drafted and went to Vietnam. He ended up coming home in a box. Gram said Mom was a good girl until she lied and said she was going to college orientation, but hitchhiked her way to the Woodstock music festival instead. Gram would never have let her do that, so that's why she had to lie. Woodstock was where all the hippies went to listen to music, do LSD and fornicate. I don't know what fornicate means but that's what I heard Gram say when she didn't think I was listening.

My Dad was there at Woodstock, too, because that's how I got here. I think it's weird that I don't know who he is. I don't even have a picture of him. I heard Gram say he must have been one of those filthy, dirty hippies who got my Mom in trouble and lead her astray. She was supposed to go to college at SUNY Binghamton, but had to leave after her first semester because she was pregnant with me.

I don't talk to people about my Mom. Everyone else I know has a mom who lives with them. Even Christopher who sits next to me at school. I don't like him. He picks boogers out of his nose and eats them, and he is always farting. And he copies off of my paper all the time. I told Gram, but she said I just needed to turn the other cheek and be nice to him because it is the Christian thing to do. I don't understand why Jesus would want me to have to smell Christopher's farts. Anyway, it's not fair that Christopher has a real mom and I don't. I saw his mom once at a school assembly. She is about 300 pounds and only has one tooth, but she was there and my Mom was not. Gram goes to all my school assemblies. I guess I will write about Gram. She's the only real mom I've ever had.

May 17th, 1981

Today is my 11th birthday. Gram is having a birthday party for me. She let me give out invitations at school and church. She said I could have 10 people. My best friend Julia is coming and she gets to sleep over. Julia lives in town. Her father is the mayor. Her mom is really nice; she makes us the best chocolate chip cookies. Julia and I spend almost every Saturday together, either at her house or mine. I tell her all my secrets and she doesn't blab them ever.

Anyway, for my party Gram made me a chocolate devil's food cake with chocolate frosting because that is my favorite. She and Gramps got me a present but I have to wait until the party to open it. I wonder what it is? I couldn't figure it out from the shape of the package. I really want a puppy, but they said I'm too young to take care of it. I don't think so, but grown-ups always get to make these decisions. When I grow up I am going to get a puppy and nobody will tell me I can't.

Oh, and Sunflower's card came today. She looks the same as last year in the picture she sent. She looks happy but she wrote that she misses me and wants to come back to see me. She is waiting to raise the bread. That doesn't make any sense. Gram bakes bread sometimes and it doesn't take that long to rise. And what difference does it make if she has bread or not? I don't think she'll really come. She has said she would come before but never does. I'll believe it when I see it.

Well, that's it for now. Gram is calling and she wants me to get dressed and ready for the party.

June 16th, 1981

Today is the last day of school and summer vacation has arrived! I can't wait to go to the lake. Gram signed me up for swimming lessons again and Julia's mom signed her up too, so we get to go together. In September I'll be in sixth grade. Middle school! We switch classes and have different teachers all day. Miss Rumson recommended me for the Gifted and Talented class because I did really well on some state test we had to take. I think it will be fun, though, because I heard the teacher is really nice.

We have to do a summer reading assignment and write a book report to bring on the first day of school. I don't think it's fair to have homework in the summer. But I don't need to think about that now. Now that school is out I can stay up later, except for the days I have swim. I have to be at class at nine in the morning.

Julia's older brother is a lifeguard. His name is James. He's 16. Julia says girls are always calling the house. He's pretty popular and all the teenage girls are in love with him, but I don't see what the fuss is. James is nice and pretty good-looking I guess, but I've known him for so long he is like a brother to me. He gives me piggy back rides sometimes. He also listens to a lot of loud rock music. He really likes some band called Led Zeppelin and a band called Leonerd Skinnerd (not sure how to spell that) and some other band named after a color, I think Pink Floyd. He listens to their album about a wall. I don't get what is so interesting about a wall. And it's a double album.

I like all kinds of music. Even church music. That's because I like to sing. Sometimes I pretend I'm a singer and I use my hairbrush as a microphone. But that's only when nobody is around. Except Julia. She never makes fun of me and she likes to sing too. We pretend we're famous singers and live together in an apartment in New York City. We both love the musical *Godspell*.

Well, time to go for now.

September 3rd, 1981

I can't believe summer is already over. I got in trouble for waiting until the last minute to do my book report. But I got it done. I think I did a good job. We had our middle school orientation. My teachers seem nice. I really like my Gifted and Talented class teacher. It sounds like we are going to do a lot of fun projects. There are only eight of us in the class. Julia didn't make it but I know most of the kids and they are OK. At least Christopher isn't in it. I don't think he is in any of my classes, thank God. Oops, I mean the Lord. Gram hates when I say God instead of the Lord. I don't see what difference it makes. I am thanking him after all.

Now that we're in middle school we get to take Music as a separate class. I don't have to share it with Art and

Library. The Music teacher is funny. He is this old fashioned guy who used to live on Long Island but moved here. He has a very strong Long Island accent and waves his hands around a lot when he talks. The boys say he is a homo. I don't think that's very nice. Gram says homosexuality is a sin.

Well, I have to go get school supplies with Gram. She sure has had to do a lot of shopping for me. I grew so much during the summer that she had to buy me all new clothes at the Kmart. Some of the rich kids get to go to the Middletown Mall. They wear designer jeans like Calvin Kleins and make fun of people like me who wear stuff from Kmart. Gram says not to listen to them, that they are just spoiled brats. I just ignore them and they leave me alone. I'm not fun to pick on I guess because I really don't care what they think. They are just a bunch of stupid girls. They are boy crazy, too. They make such fools out of themselves around the boys. The boys pretend to annoy them and act like jerks. There is one boy in my class, Harold, who makes fart noises with his armpit and hand to make everybody laugh. What an idiot. I don't think he's funny at all. But at least they don't smell.

Maybe Gram will let me look at Halloween costumes while we are out. I want to be Sandy from *Grease*.

November 1st, 1981

Well, I am officially sick from eating Halloween candy. Julia and I went trick-or-treating last night. I didn't get to be Sandy. Gram did not want me being that hussy. So I just went as a hobo. This weekend the Methodist church youth group is going to visit a haunted house in Slate Hill. I get to go this year because I'm in middle school now. I hope the older boys don't play tricks on us like they did to the girls last year. But if they do I'm ready. Sean Oliver got in big trouble last year for pulling one girl into a dark room and pretending to be a zombie.

Parent/teacher conferences are coming up. I'm sure Gram

will go. They started scheduling them at night because so many parents work during the day. I'm not worried; my grades have been good. Gram said if I keep up the good work she'll get me a guitar for Christmas. I saw an Epiphone in the music store on Main Street that I really like. I've been starting to write song lyrics, too. I don't get to be in the school talent show until I'm in eighth grade, but I do get to perform in the chorus.

The boys in music still make fun of our teacher, Mr. Schumann, behind his back. I like him though, even if he is weird and says dumb things when he is mad at us like, "I must be in an opium dream." What does that mean? He does know a lot about music and we get to have two recitals. One before Christmas break and one in May. He gave me a solo for the one at Christmas!

Speaking of Christmas, Julia is going skiing in Vermont and she invited me and Gram and Gramps said yes. We are leaving the day after Christmas. I've never been snow skiing before. I have tried water skiing at the lake. I got up a few times but always with two skis.

Would you believe Sunflower wrote and said she might try to come home for Christmas? As if. I guess she finally baked her bread.

1982

January 15th, 1982

We just had a huge snow storm and school has been closed for almost a week. We were hardly back from Christmas break. I've gotten to go sledding every day with Julia. We had a great time in Vermont. We stayed at a ski resort and it took a while to get there. Julia is a really good skier so I didn't get to spend much time with her because I had to learn how to ski and never got off the bunny slope. I fell down a lot and people don't look where they are going which drives me crazy. Most days I ended up back at the lodge drinking hot chocolate. I made it down the hill without falling on my last day.

Both Gram and Gramps came to see my recital. Of course, Sunflower never made it for that or Christmas. She sent me a card and a macramé bracelet she made me. Like I am going to wear some dumb hippie bracelet. She apologized for not being able to come and said something about moving to California to get her head together and attend some EST retreat. I have no idea what EST is. All I can think of is some room where a bunch of hippies sit around and predict the future. Oh wait, that's ESP … oh well. What a weirdo I have for a mother. She said she hopes to make it out here by my birthday. Uh huh.

But most importantly, I got my guitar! It is beautiful! It's an Epiphone 6-string acoustic like I wanted. I've learned three chords so far. I have a book that shows them so I just copy what it shows with my fingers. I've started to make up some songs, but I don't know if I like them yet. I haven't played them for anyone. I really want guitar lessons. Gram is trying to find a guitar teacher for me. She's been asking at church. I hope I don't get a teacher who makes me play hymns. Hymns on a guitar? Ugh.

I can't believe sixth grade is almost half over. We've been doing this really cool project in Gifted and Talented class. We call it G&T class for short. Since we are studying Ancient Greece, we are making a replica of Athens. I'm making the Parthenon. We have to use clay. I have a partner that I work with; his name is Kyle. He just moved here from Maryland. His dad got transferred. He has six brothers and sisters. His mom is a housewife; I guess it's a lot of work taking care of all those kids.

She makes all of them lunch, every day, before they go to school. Kyle seems to like peanut butter and jelly. He eats it every day. He is very shy, so I don't know much about him except that he is smart and has really nice pale blue eyes and straight, thin brown hair. The popular girls like him and try to flirt with him all the time but he thinks they are stupid and boring. I like him for that. I only see him in G&T class. He doesn't go to our church so he's not in youth group. He's Catholic and goes to St. Stephen The First Martyr Parish. That's a long name. He just calls it St. Stephen's. I also am in Music with Kyle. He doesn't act like a jerk like the other boys, but I don't really get to talk to him in that class because I have to sit with the girls in the alto section. Julia is a soprano so she doesn't sit with me either.

We are just starting to learn our songs for the spring recital. It's going to be right around my birthday. We're going to have an afternoon performance and an evening performance. The afternoon one is for the whole school and the evening one is for parents and family. The band has one, too. I thought about taking Band, but I didn't like any of the instruments that were available. I would have had to play the trombone or French horn. I'd rather just play my guitar anyway. Well, time to go. Gram wants me to set the table for dinner.

February 14th, 1982

Today is Valentine's Day. It snowed but not enough to close school. Kyle and I talk a lot now and we sit together at lunch. Julia is mad at me. She thinks I dropped her for

Kyle. I told her that's not true, but she doesn't believe me and now she started hanging around with the popular girls and she started a rumor that Kyle and I went to second base. I hate her. Kyle and I are just friends but he got me a Valentine. I was so happy because I really like him, and even though we are just friends, I like him that way. I can only see him in school because Gram says I am too young to have a boyfriend. He wants to hear me play guitar.

Oh, I finally got a guitar teacher, and not a church person either. Gram found a music teacher from the high school who gives lessons. He comes to my house. I've learned a few songs so far, but I haven't played mine for anyone yet. My songs are private. But I'd play them for Kyle. Now I just have to figure out a way to do that outside of school. We were thinking that when it gets warmer we could hang out in the park by the library after school, and maybe Saturdays, and I could tell Gram that I was going to the library to study. Except I can't bring my guitar to school so I would have to go home to get it and of course Gram would ask why I needed to bring a guitar to the library.

Kyle likes music, too. He's also in the Chorus – oh, I said that already. Well anyway, he has a good voice so sometimes we sing together at recess. I am going to invite him to one of our youth group trips. We can bring a guest and Gram will let me do that. I guess if Kyle and I want to see each other on Saturdays that's the best I can do.

March 19th, 1982

Gram sat me down to have a talk today. She's worried about me because she thinks I don't have any friends. I guess Kyle doesn't count because I only see him in school. Julia and I aren't friends anymore and Gram keeps asking me about that. I just tell her that Julia is a snob who hangs out with the popular girls (which is pretty much the truth anyway). So she told me she is looking into day camp for me in the summer

to get me to socialize more. How will I get to see Kyle then?
I was planning on going to the lake like always and meeting
him there. I don't want to go to some stupid camp even if they
do have swimming and horseback riding. Maybe I can find a
way to talk her out of it.

Kyle and I made a plan to meet at the library after school
Mondays, Tuesdays and Thursdays. I have guitar lessons on
Wednesdays. He has "family game night" on Fridays. He
wants to invite me to that but said his parents said it's just
for family. Anyway, I told Gram I'm going to the library to
study on those days and she believes me. Since I can't do my
homework at home now, Kyle and I do our homework first
when we get there and then we go to the park to hang out. It
stays light longer so we have some time before we have to go
home for dinner. We hold hands now and he kissed me on the
lips for the first time last week. But I didn't do anything slutty
like French kiss with a tongue. We hug a lot though. I like the
way it feels when we're close like that. I can't wait until we're
older and can hang out together for real.

April 15th, 1982

I've been so busy I have not had time to write. The days
are longer now so I get more time to spend with Kyle. And it's
spring break so I made up some story to tell Gram about how I
have to write a book report for school. So I'm carrying around
a book all week just so I can hang out with Kyle at the park by
the library. We spend a lot of time kissing and hugging but we
have to be careful because we don't want anyone to tell Gram
and Gramps or his parents. Gram is still talking about day
camp. I told Kyle to ask his parents if he can go too. He did,
but he doesn't have an answer from them yet. I am hoping
he does. My birthday is in a month and I'll be 12. Almost a
teenager. I wonder what Sunflower will send me this year.
She left the pig place in New Mexico and lives in California
now. She told Gram and Gramps that she is working in a

café and trying to save money to come back home. Gram said they would send money but she wants to pay her own way. I'm not sure how I would feel seeing her after all these years. Would I have to call her Mom? Or would I call her Sunflower? Anyway, she says she is sober now and going to a 12-Step program and has a sponsor who she has to call every day to report that she is sober. They have a big celebration when she is sober for 90 days. She told Gram that she isn't doing drugs anymore and that now she does yoga. I talk to Kyle about my Mom. I can tell him anything. He thinks it's cool that she was a hippie because his mom is a regular old mom/housewife. Like Gram. Gram told me that next year when I'm in seventh grade I can have boys who are friends, but not boyfriends. At least Kyle and I will be able to hang out without sneaking around. Well, I'm going to the library now, at least that's what I told Gram. It's a nice day so I am going to hang out with Kyle.

May 1st, 1982

Has it really been two weeks since I last wrote in here? I guess that's because I've been so busy. We've been having extra rehearsals after school for the spring chorus concert at the end of this month. Mr. Schumann gave me another solo. I don't care what the other kids say about him, he is really nice. I am going to sing "Day by Day" from *Godspell.* I am so excited! I also get to play my guitar as part of it. My first time playing in public! I'm nervous. But I'm also kind of sad that Julia and I are not friends anymore because we could have sung a duet. We used to have so much fun singing that song together. She has a special part in another song, but she was jealous I got picked again for the solo so she started up a rumor saying that Gram demanded that I get the solo and that's why I got it. Some kids actually believed her because she hangs out with the popular crowd now. I don't care. I'm the one who got the solo after all.

Kyle is so proud of me. I've been practicing in front of him after chorus rehearsals. I just tell Gram to get me from school a little later than she needs to. Plus, now she is letting me go to the library with Kyle to study on Saturdays since I am so busy during the week. I still am not allowed to go anywhere else with him, but Gram lets me talk to him on the phone. She said if I keep my grades up she'll get me my own line for my birthday since nobody can call the house anymore because the line is always busy. Well, if she would let me hang out with Kyle more then the phone would be free. Oh well.

He's been writing song lyrics. They are really good. We are trying to find a way to convince Gram to let us be together more so we can write songs together. I haven't French kissed him yet, but I can tell it is going to happen soon. I really, really like him. Oh, and my birthday and Mother's Day are soon. I've gotten used to giving my Gram Mother's Day cards, but now that Paula/Sunflower/whatever has been making more of an effort to stay in touch with me, Gram wants me to get her a card, too. Sunflower's living somewhere on the coast of Oregon. She's not a waitress anymore. Now she's a secretary and is making more money so she's still saying she's coming here. Yeah right. She's been writing me letters a lot more. Gram makes me write her back. I don't know what to say to her. I don't know her. I ask her what Oregon is like. She says it's nice but they get a lot of rain. Well, that's it for now, got stuff to do, plus Kyle's going to call soon.

May 18th, 1982

You will never believe this. The woman who calls herself my Mom did not show up for my birthday. But she sent me a card, a long letter and a gold locket with a picture of her holding me when I was a baby. All I sent her for Mother's Day was a Hallmark card with my name. It was really weird to see that picture. I had never seen it before. She looks happy holding me. She has a smile on her face and is looking down at me. Her hair looks brushed and neat and she looks like a normal young woman from what I can see. I'm sleeping, in her arms, in a pink crocheted blanket. I'm not sure how I feel about seeing that picture. I haven't worn the locket yet. I don't understand how the woman in that picture could leave me. I look so little and helpless. What kind of person does that to her baby? And now that she got sober, she wants us to have this relationship like nothing happened. Gram says it's Christian to forgive and turn the other cheek. I'm starting to think I should become an atheist, but I don't say that to Gram. She'll never let me hang out with Kyle if I say that. I did get a phone for my birthday, with my own private line. It's one of those powder blue princess phones, with a dial. The only person who calls me though is Kyle; oh, and the woman who calls herself my Mom. It is really weird to speak to her. Even weirder than writing to her. She tells me all about her day, which is really boring. There is no way I'll work in an office when I get older. I'm going to sing and play guitar. Kyle is going to write lyrics and we are going to make an album and get played on the radio. I'm going to be somebody famous, not a loser like my mother. I don't care if she is getting her life back together. So what? She's just a boring secretary. She could have gone to college but instead she ran off to the pig farm or whatever that place was called. Gram sent her a picture of me. She can't believe how old I've gotten. What did she think, I'd remain a baby forever, waiting for her to come back? Please. Oh well, enough about her. I have to practice for the concert. It's coming up really soon.

June 12th, 1982

We had the concert and it went really well. Everybody loved my solo and guitar playing. Even the popular kids. Julia was so jealous. Gram and Gramps came for the evening performance. Then we had a big pizza party when it was over.

I was just glad I had an excuse to be with Kyle. Speaking of that, Gram is sending me to that dumb camp. Thank God it is only for the month of July. It's a Methodist camp, but at least we get to do some normal things like swim and play softball, and I do want to go horseback riding. I'll be in a group with a bunch of other 12-year-old girls who are from all over Orange county. I hope they're nice. Not that it really matters to me, this is all Gram's idea. At least my swimming will improve. I am trying to be really good, because Gram said if I behave like a mature young lady, she will let me have Kyle over – when I am not in school, church or camp and she or Gramps is home AND in the house. And, we have to stay in the living room. Under no circumstances can he go upstairs to my bedroom. And we have to have a space between us when we sit on the couch. Oh, brother! How are we going to kiss now? I'll have to figure something out.

July 15th, 1982

Well it happened. I got my period today. Right when I was about to be at bat in a softball game at camp. It was so embarrassing. I didn't realize what was going on at first. I just started feeling the worst cramps I have ever felt in my body. Thank God the counselor let me go to the bathroom. When I saw what happened, I just ran to the infirmary. The nurse helped me and asked if I wanted her to call my Gram to take me home. I said yes. So Gram came and got me. She put me to bed when we got home with a hot water bottle for my belly and sat on the edge of the bed. She then proceeded to have "The Talk" with me. You know, the one about the birds and the bees. Now I don't know why she didn't think I knew where babies come from. She had to sign a permission slip for me to go to that stupid school assembly where we watched a movie called *"You Are a Woman Now."* The boys had a separate assembly and a different movie. Kyle said it was about wet dreams(?) and penises. Our movie was all about how our ovaries work and how eggs get fertilized. But they did really show how boys were involved. The popular girls were all laughing and goofing around and acting silly. They made fun of the whole thing, got in trouble and all had to serve detention. Anyway, so Gram starts having "The Talk" with me, you know, about how I am a woman and how boys will want to do things to me and as a good Christian girl I should not let them. I am supposed to save myself for marriage and not be a fallen woman like my mother. She went on and on about how I must remain pure and a virgin. All I wanted to do was go to sleep. My cramps were killing me and the last thing I wanted to think about was having a penis in my hoo-hoo. Finally, I guess I convinced her that I was not going to become the town whore and that Kyle and I were just friends. Of course, I didn't tell her about the kissing. Now I have to be extra careful. Especially because camp will be over soon and I need to be able to be allowed to go to the lake. I can't wait to be free and see Kyle during the day and play guitar and sing. If Gram thinks I'm wild she won't let me go to the lake. So I am being really good and doing all my chores without being asked and not giving her any lip. It's not easy but it's worth it.

August 31st, 1982

Well, I did it! I managed to get to the lake almost every day to be with Kyle and Gram didn't suspect a thing. We found a really nice private spot to be together in the woods. We spend a lot of time making out but we also are writing songs together and practicing them. This has been the best month of my life. It's hard to go home at night. I wish I could spend every minute with Kyle. I love him so much. Gram took me for back-to-school shopping yesterday. I grew a lot this summer, I'm almost 5'5"! My doctor said I will probably be about 5'6" or 5'7". And I have boobs now! So we had to buy bras. Who invented those things? It had to be a man. They are so annoying. But if I don't wear one I'll get called a slut so I guess I have to. Oh, and now I have hair down there and under my arms and Gram is letting me shave my legs. The boys are starting to notice me now. They make stupid comments, but everyone knows I am with Kyle. Julia thinks we're doing it. Gross. She's such an ass. She is a real flirt, too, but flat as a board so none of the boys will ask her out. Serves her right. It turns out that Kyle and I have three classes together besides G&T! I am so happy. Plus, we have the same lunch period. Seventh grade is going to be awesome.

October 12th, 1982

We have off from school today since it's Columbus Day. I've been so busy I haven't had time to write. Now that I'm in seventh grade we get massive amounts of homework. Now I really do need to go to the library every day. But I don't have to hide Kyle from Gram anymore, she trusts me with him. Kyle and I go to the library every day after school except Friday, when he comes over after school. It's getting cold now so it's harder to sneak away and find places to be alone. We do though. I am going to get him something special for Christmas. I'm saving my allowance. Our school is having a Halloween dance. It's for seventh and eighth grade only. Of course I am going with Kyle. And, of course, Gram volunteered to be a chaperone. We have to come in costume. Kyle and I are trying to think of something we can be together. We want to go as Carly Simon and James Taylor so I can bring my guitar and we can go off and play and sing. If they let us. Neither of us is interested in dancing, unless it is a slow dance and then they told us we have to be an arm's length apart. Really? How lame. I got a really strange letter from my Mom. I'm trying to get used to calling her that. She wants me to call her Mom. Not Sunflower or Paula. Anyway, it was this long letter all about how sorry she is for being a bad mom and as part of her program she has to make amends to those she has harmed and so she is making amends to me. She apologized for leaving me when I was a little baby and not being a responsible parent. She said she knows she was wrong and only thinking of herself, and hopes I will forgive her. I guess that's supposed to make up for everything. She has been sober for a year, she said, and is looking forward to coming home and being a real mom. Gram thinks she's serious this time. I don't know how I feel about that. My Mom wants to be home for Christmas, but she doesn't think she can take a week off from work. She said no matter what, she will be home by my birthday. I told Kyle. He thinks it's cool. I don't. I like my life the way it is. I don't know if I want to live with her. How do I go from not having a mom to all of a sudden having one live in my house? Will Gram still go to my school concerts? Will Mom be going to church with us? She says she doesn't go to church. She says she has her own higher power, whatever that means. But I know Gram, and if my Mom lives in this house she is going to have to go to church. Personally, I don't want to go to church anymore either so maybe having my Mom here would be a good thing. But we'll see if she really comes. She hasn't yet, sober or not.

December 1st, 1982

Thanksgiving came and went but my Mom was not here. She is not going to be here for Christmas, either. She still calls to talk to me every week. She is working a lot of overtime to save money to move back to New York. She says that she needs more than she thought because she doesn't have a job lined up yet, but as soon as she does she will be here. I am not holding my breath. I'm getting used to her voice though. I am going to send her a Christmas present this year. Gram said she would help me pick something out.

Gram really seems to like Kyle! Thank God, because we spend almost every day together. We've written two songs together. We played them for Gram and Gramps and they liked them. Sometimes I go to Kyle's house. It's pretty loud over there because of all his brothers and sisters. His mom is nice though. His dad is quiet and works a lot, but is nice. He shares a room with his brother, so we usually hang out in the family room in the basement and watch MTV. I want us to make a music video. We both tried out for the play, since we're allowed to be in it now that we're in seventh grade. It's *You're A Good Man Charlie Brown*.

Kyle is Linus. I'm Peppermint Patty. Julia didn't get a part. So now she and her friends are saying the play is dumb. I saw her sneaking a cigarette behind the gym the other day. She's starting to dress like a slut, too. She thinks she is so cool. I think she's stupid. Kyle says he agrees with me, but she still flirts with him. That really makes me angry but he says not to worry, that he doesn't like her.

1983

January 16th, 1983

Well, Christmas came and went. It was OK. My Mom got me a really cool present. A Sony Walkman and some tapes. Somehow she knew that I loved Joan Jett so that was one of them. She also got me The Cars and Squeeze. I think it is kind of cool that she remembered what music I listen to. I really like New Wave.

Something is going on with Gram and Gramps. I'm not sure what happened, but I was listening in to a phone call with Gram and my Mom and heard something very strange. Mom was explaining why she was not coming home for Christmas and how she would be here for my birthday. She informed Gram that she was moving back East and was actively looking for a job. Gram told her that she should move back in with us, since I was happy here. Which is true. But then my Mom said something very strange. She told Gram that would never happen because of what Gramps did, and that as soon as she could she was going to get an apartment and take me with her! I don't want to move! It better not be in another town. But my Mom never goes through with anything anyway. I will believe it when I see it. Besides, Gram knows this is my home. She told my Mom that. And then Gram got very angry and said that the Lord wants us to forgive others their trespasses. My Mom said she would never forgive him and Gram knows what he did and is just an enabler, whatever that is. Gram told her the conversation was over and hung up. She hung up on my Mom. She never does that. Gram is the most polite person I know.

Then things really got weird. The next day Gram put a lock on my bedroom door. She told me that now that I am a woman, I need my privacy. Then she told me that I should lock it every night after I go to bed. Huh? I tried to ask her why; I mean, what if I need to go to the bathroom in the middle of the night? I have to unlock the door to get out. And who does she think is going to get in? So when I asked her she just said, "Do as I say and don't ask any questions." Right, okay, yeah sure. So now I lock my bedroom door. I don't ask any more questions because I don't want her to ground me from Kyle. She finally lets me spend pretty much all of my free time with him so I have to be careful. We go to his house most of the time anyway. Gram thinks it is OK because his mom is home and he has so many brothers and sisters. But what she doesn't know is that he moved his bedroom down to the basement and his mother is so busy that she doesn't pay attention when I come over. She thinks we just watch MTV and play guitar. Which we do, but we spend a lot of time making out. I think he wants to go to second, but I am not sure if I am ready.

Oh yeah, so back to Gram and Gramps. So Gramps has hired people to do most of the farm work because he has a bad back. He spends most of the day watching TV and drinking beer. He still goes to Poker Night, but that's about it. A lot of the time he passes out in front of the TV and sleeps through dinner. Gram always leaves a plate for him in the fridge to heat up, but sometimes it is still there in the morning and Gramps is still on the couch. I don't like being around him when he drinks. He isn't an angry drunk and he doesn't beat me (like some other kids' parents I know) but before he passes out, he gets kind of goofy and says dumb things. Like the other day, I caught him staring at me and he told me I am turning into a damn fine woman. Gram heard and she was pissed. She told me to stay away from him when he is in his cups, I guess that means when he is drinking beer. But she puts up with the drinking. We never invite anyone over anymore, and Gram won't leave me alone with him. The whole thing is creepy. I think he needs help. Gram says he struggles with demons from his time serving in the war. She says he drinks to forget and that a man is the king of his castle and it is her job to obey her husband. Even if he is going to drink himself to death? I haven't told anyone about this, not even Kyle. I don't want anyone to know how weird our house is.

So I try to stay out of the house as much as I can, except when I have to help Gram with chores. I offered to clean house on Saturday mornings because then she lets me spend the rest of the day with Kyle as long as either she or Kyle's parents bring me home at 9 p.m. She never lets Gramps drive to get me. He's usually passed out by then anyway. I also still go to church with Gram on Sunday because I know where my bread is buttered. The more I do what Gram wants the more I get to be with Kyle. And that is all I care about. Well, that and the play. It's in March and we have a lot of rehearsals after school. Julia and her dorky friends walk by the auditorium and say stupid things. She still has a crush on Kyle so they call his name out. He just ignores them.

February 14th, 1983

Today was the best day ever. Gram let me spend it with Kyle because it was Valentine's Day. Since it is Monday and a school night I had to be home by seven and show that my homework was done. But, the important thing is that I got to spend it with Kyle. He gave me an engraved bracelet with our names on it! So we were making out and I let him go to second, but only over my shirt. He told me he loved me! I told him I loved him too. Life is the best when I am with Kyle.

March 17th, 1983

So the play is this week. Gram says she and Gramps are going; I hope he doesn't embarrass me. He does seem to be drinking a bit less, but still… I don't want him showing up drunk and saying something stupid in front of everybody. We have dress rehearsal tonight and then the performance for the school tomorrow, and then tomorrow night and Saturday night for parents and the community. I think it's going to be good. And then, get this, Julia actually invited Kyle to a boy/ girl party at her house over spring break, which is the first week of April. I can't believe she had the nerve to do that. He told her he would only go if he could bring me. Except I don't want to go to Julia's party. I think he knows that but he was hoping she would say no and that would be the end of it. But then she said OK. And now she's being overly nice to me and her friends are, too. I don't trust her. I know all of the kids who are going; it's the popular crowd and the girls are all Julia's snotty friends who parade around in their Calvin Kleins and think they are so hot. The boys are mostly the jocks from the recreational football team. Julia is on the recreational cheerleading squad with her dumb friends, I forgot to mention that.

So anyway, I know this is going to be a make out party with kissing games like Spin The Bottle and Seven Minutes In Heaven. She's just hoping she gets to make out with Kyle, which really makes me mad. I don't want to see her kiss him! And if they end up in the closet I don't know what I will do. And then do I have to kiss some dumb boy who slobbers like a fish? Eww! I don't know why I agreed to go. I guess I do anything to be with Kyle. Gram is all excited because she thinks Julia and I are friends again. Right. Whatever.

I've been working on some song lyrics and writing music for them. I haven't shared them with Kyle yet. My Mom wants to hear my songs. She asked me to play one over the phone but I feel weird doing that. I still can't get used to her being in my life. Everything just feels weird these days.

And Gram is insisting Gramps go to the doctor. Gramps hates doctors and he won't go. She is worried because his eyes are looking yellow, he has no appetite and is tired all the time. She wants him to stop drinking. I thought he was drinking less, but I saw him hiding beer bottles out by the barn. Does he really think Gram is that dumb? But she sees what she wants to see. Anyway, I have to go do my homework. I have gotten behind with play practice.

April 10th, 1983

So the play went really well. Gramps behaved himself and Julia and her friends actually clapped and congratulated me. I think it is because she just wants to make sure Kyle comes to the party. She is such a phony. Oh yeah, and that party. Well, we went. And sure enough it was a make-out party. We started with Spin The Bottle. Of course I didn't get Kyle, and of course Julia did. I swear that bottle was fixed. I was not going to let any of those boys get a tongue in my mouth and they didn't. One of them snuck in beer. After Seven Minutes In Heaven (Julia did not get Kyle, thank God) they turned down the lights and passed out the beers. I tried some but it just tasted bitter to me. Then people paired up to make out. Julia knew she wouldn't get Kyle so she made a big show of making out with one of the football guys to look cool. So we were all paired up and then because it was too quiet Julia's Mom opened the door to the basement and called down and we all had to stop what we were doing and hide the beer. And of course she put the lights on. So that was the end of that. She said from now on the door stays open and that she wanted to hear talking or everyone had to go home. You know what, that would have been fine with me. I would rather just go be alone with Kyle anyway. I didn't want to go to the party in the first place and I am not sure why Kyle did. He's not friends with any of those kids. I didn't say anything because I didn't want to get in a fight. I wonder if he secretly has a crush on Julia. She has boobs now. But I heard a rumor that she stuffs her bra. That would've been funny if she ended up in the closet with one of those boys and he found out for sure! But it could just be a rumor. She got in a fight with one of her dumb friends and to get back at her that girl started a rumor that she stuffs. Whatever.

Gram scheduled a doctor appointment for Gramps. They've been fighting about this lately but somehow Gram won. I think Gramps just gave in because he didn't feel like being nagged and now he can't drive because the last time he did he got a DWI. I'm still worried about him. I think Gram is right, he does not seem well. She still won't let him be alone with me and I still have to lock my door. I am beginning to think that she thinks he may do something to me when he is drunk. That creeps me out. Ugh, I don't want to think about it. I think it is gross to even think about him doing it with Gram.

May 9th, 1983

Yesterday was Mother's Day. I got Gram a card and flowers and we went out for brunch after church. Gramps stayed home. Then we called my Mom. I had gotten her a card and a scarf. She said she really liked my gift. She also said that she had her plane tickets and would be here on my birthday. She said she gave notice at her job and let her landlord know she was leaving. She is going to come for a week and look for an apartment near her new job. She is going to work for AT&T in Morristown, NJ. I don't know what that means for me. Am I going to move to another state with her? I listened in on the extension when she was talking to Gram. She told Gram that I'm her responsibility and that she wants me to live with her, especially since Gram is getting older and Gramps is sick. Oh yeah, he went to the doctor. He has cirrhosis? Some kind of problem with his liver. It's fatal. Gram is going to have to spend a lot of time taking care of him. He is on a bunch of medicines and has to go to doctor appointments and stop drinking. We no longer have alcohol in the house and Gram hides the keys to the car. The doctor said if he can't stop drinking on his own he will have to go to detox. Gramps doesn't want to go to AA because he doesn't want to sit in a room with a bunch of ex-drunks telling him what to do. He stopped drinking after the doctor's appointment and then had something called withdrawal. His hands were shaking, he was throwing up and feeling pretty sick. Gram was really worried; she was going to take him back to the doctor or the

ER but then after a couple of days it went away. Now he's just tired all the time and cranky. I think I liked him better when he was drinking. Now I can never watch TV. He won't even give up the remote. Gram just humors him and lets him watch what he wants. She is basically like his slave. It makes me mad. I am worried about her and am trying to help out more. If my Mom makes me move who will help Gram? Gram is very proud though. She says that the Lord will provide and that we all have our crosses to bear.

I asked her about whether I have to move. She said she doesn't want me to and that she will talk my Mom out of it. I hope so. I don't want to move to New Jersey. How will I see Kyle and who will help Gram? I was looking forward to spending the summer at the lake with Kyle. School will be over next month. I want to at least spend the summer here. I am not big on church anymore, but I have been praying every night. And I make sure to go on Sundays. Please God, don't make me move. I told Kyle what my Mom said. He is upset. He doesn't want me to move either. When I am not helping Gram I am spending as much time as I can with Kyle. Sometimes he has to come to my house and we have to be good. It's hard, but sometimes we'll sneak out to the barn for a little while. It's better than nothing, I guess. Plus, I want to keep him away from Julia. After the party she stopped being nice to me and is back to being a bitch. She keeps showing up where ever Kyle is and trying to flirt with him. I hate her!

May 22nd, 1983

So I turned 13 last Tuesday. And it finally happened. Gram had called the school and left a message that I should come straight home after school. I got really worried, I thought maybe Gramps passed away. So I went straight home and opened the door and there was a woman sitting on the living room couch. She had shoulder-length strawberry blonde hair that was pulled back in a barrette. She was wearing a business

suit and looked like somebody's mom. And she was. Mine.
My mother, here in the flesh in my living room. Then she got
up and gave me a big hug. I hugged her back; what else could
I do, but I swear I thought I was going to faint. After all these
years here she was. She told me that she did everything she
could to be here, in the flesh for my birthday, especially now
because I was a teenager. Gram was grinning from ear to ear
and even Gramps was in a good mood. And Kyle was sitting
there as well! They had made dinner reservations for us at a
restaurant in town and had invited Kyle, but told him not to
tell me because it was a surprise.

I just sat there with my mouth open. I did not know what to
say. Here was this woman who actually looked like a normal
mom, not a Sunflower or Paula or whatever. She told us that
she was now gainfully employed at AT&T in New Jersey in
Morristown, which is about an hour from here. She had her
final interview today and would start work next Monday.
She had also rented a two-bedroom apartment in a town near
Morristown called Persnickety (Well, that's not the real name,
but it sounds like Persnickety) and was moving there over
Memorial Day weekend. Until then she was staying with us.
Since I was in her old room, she would be staying with me.
Fortunately, I have a trundle bed so we both had a place to
sleep. Then she announced to all in the room that I would be
moving in with her as soon as I finished school at the end of
June. When I heard that I really did almost faint. I looked at
Kyle, who looked just as shocked as me. Gram and Gramps
just sat there. Are they really going to let this happen? That
was my first thought. I am moving from the only home I
have known to a place called Persnickety? And she took me
there over this past weekend. What an ugly place! It is one
of those garden apartment complexes, on a highway near the
interstate. And it's painted this awful purplish pink color
that looks like Pepto Bismol. Who would paint anything that
color? Anyway, her apartment (I refuse to call it mine) has
two bedrooms, one bathroom, a living room / dining area and

a kitchen. You have to walk up a flight of stairs to get to it and there is an apartment underneath it. There are a bunch of different buildings that are all painted the same disgusting Pepto Bismol color. In the middle of the complex is a pool. That Woman (which is what I call Paula/Sunflower now) thought I would be excited about that. Like I would really rather spend time at a pool in Persnickety instead of at the lake with Kyle. Is she serious?

I have been in shock the whole week. I hardly ate anything at my birthday dinner and barely touched the cake we had when we got home. All I wanted was to go to my room and cry, and I couldn't do that with everybody there and especially with That Woman sleeping in my room on top of everything. Her stuff is all over the room too. It feels like an alien invaded. I haven't been able to concentrate on anything in school and I have deliberately not come home after school because I don't want to see her. All I have been doing is crying to Kyle. He holds me and lets me cry, but he doesn't know what to say because he is not happy about this either.

Oh, and she gave me tickets to see The Cars for my birthday, but just for me and her. She didn't get one for Kyle. So now I have to go see one of our favorite bands with That Woman. A real mom would know me better and care about how I feel and not make me move to Persnickety. I just can't believe this is happening. I have less than a month to spend with Kyle, so I told Gram I was going to spend most of it with him. Gramps' health is pretty stable right now so she does not need as much help. That Woman wants me to spend weekends with her until I move in. I refused and told Gram there was no way I was going to do that. Gram said she was going to talk to That Woman, but That Woman was my legal guardian (Gram never got legal guardianship for me) and she was sorry but I needed to go live with That Woman (well, she didn't put it like that, but still). I was like, but what about you and Gramps? What about Kyle? She explained that my Mom is willing to take me back for a few weekend visits and that I can see her and

Gramps and Kyle then and still go to the lake. So that makes everything better??

I usually look forward to the end of the school year but now I am dreading it. I am going to have to go to Persnickety Middle School for my eighth-grade year, and instead of graduating with all the people I know, and getting to be in the talent show, I will be in that place. Where I know nobody. I can't believe she is doing this to me. I wish she stayed on her pig farm getting stoned or whatever they do there. Now I'm starting to cry again so I'm going to stop writing and play my guitar and sing. Maybe that will make me feel better. I've been writing this in the barn by the way. It's the only place I can go to be alone when I'm home, until That Woman moves us to her apartment.

June 14th, 1983

So I spent all last weekend at That Woman's apartment. I didn't get to see Kyle once the whole weekend. That Woman (I think I will just call her TW from now on) picked me up after she finished work Friday and took me there, and there I stayed until Sunday afternoon. I was all by myself for a while on Saturday and Sunday morning because TW goes to AA meetings on both Saturday and Sunday. On Saturday I watched MTV until I got bored and then walked around the apartment complex. The pool is not open yet. They wait for school to be out. I saw some kids playing football and some kicking a soccer ball, but they just ignored me. A lot of the kids are much younger than me anyway. So TW comes home after her AA meeting and tells me that she is taking me to TGI Fridays for dinner and I can have anything I want. Big Whoop. I purposely picked the most expensive thing on the menu and she didn't even bat an eye. She just went on and on about how she was so happy she got her life together and got sober and how she is so grateful for the program. That's what she calls AA. She wants me to go to an Alateen meeting that they have in the library on Saturdays at the same time as her meeting. There is no way I am going to do that and I told her so. I am not going to sit around with a bunch of kids talking about how TW ran off to a commune and left me and about how Gramps is an alcoholic and has cirrhosis. Why would I ever want to do that? She sighed and looked disappointed but said if I change my mind to let her know. Yeah right.

Oh, and the neighbors downstairs are jerks. I saw them outside and they look normal but since they live underneath TW I can hear everything that they do. And I mean everything. And they can hear us. The husband keeps banging on his ceiling (TW's floor) and telling us to keep the noise down. What noise? MTV? It isn't that loud. And he complains about us walking on the floor. Really? How are we supposed to get around, fly? Oh, and then, he and his wife do it first thing in the morning and he howls like a train. I swear to God. I hate that apartment and I can't believe I am going to live there. I could not wait to get home Sunday. Gram asked me how things went. I said OK. What was I supposed to say, that Mr. Weirdo howls like a train at seven in the morning?

So next week I move in because school is over. Gram is letting me spend every day after school with Kyle. I can't believe I am not going to be able to be with him this summer. I don't trust TW. She cares more about her AA friends than me. And she says she'll drive me to Gram and Gramps so I can spend one weekend a month there. I was like, that's it?

Then she gave me some crap about how she knows I'm angry and she understands, but I need to get used to my new home before school starts. I can't believe this is happening. Oh, and then Julia found out I was moving, so she is flirting shamelessly with Kyle. Right in front of me. He tries to blow her off, but I can tell he kind of likes her. She started listening to the same music as us and asking him to come over and play songs for her. She told him she will be at the lake all summer. This just sucks. He promised me he was not going to cheat but she is relentless and I will be gone. He promised he would call me as much as he could, but it's long distance so I guess we'll have to write letters. Now I'm starting to cry again. I'll write more later.

July 5th, 1983

Well, here I am back at Pepto Bismol Gardens in lovely downtown Persnickety. Except there is no downtown in Persnickety. It basically is a bunch of apartments and strip malls all along Route 46. Oh, and now a bunch of office buildings are being built. Supposedly this used to be farm land. In fact, there's a section of it named after a lake and it doesn't even have a lake. I have been here since school let out and there is nothing to do all day but go to the dumb pool, which is full of little kids whose parents use the lifeguard as a babysitter. And he is some dumb guy who creeps me out because he's always staring at me. He doesn't live here but he goes to the community college. He looks like he's on steroids and he's always flexing his muscles. When I get sick of the pool I go back to the apartment and watch MTV or play my guitar and write songs. I have quite a few now, but it is not the same without Kyle.

Speaking of Kyle, I finally got to see him this past weekend. TW let me go to Gram and Gramps' house for July 4th weekend. She dropped me off on Saturday morning and stayed to take us all out to lunch. I am worried about Gram; Gramps seems to be getting worse again. I try to call her as much as I can. Anyway, I finally got to see Kyle afterwards. We spent almost the whole weekend at the lake together. It was so hard to leave and come back here. Julia was at the lake, too, and she is still flirting shamelessly with him. He says he still only wants me, but I saw him looking at her boobs in her bikini. Or what is supposed to be a bikini. She looks like a whore. I wanted to ask her how much she charged. She walked right up to him and acted like I wasn't even there. It made me really mad. And her stupid friends just do whatever she says. But Kyle stayed with me the entire time and we went off to be alone which was great. I let him go to second for real this time. He promised to write more and call as much as he can when he can get the phone. I have to call him most of the time. I don't care how much I run up TW's phone bill. It's her fault I'm here. She wants me to meet her friend's daughter. She has this AA friend who lives in town that has a daughter who is a year older than me. Her name is Alicia and she is going into ninth grade. Persnickety has two high schools and she is going to the one I will be going to, so TW thinks it would be good for me to know someone there since I will be going next year. I still haven't met anyone from the middle school. TW is going to take me there soon to register me and so I can meet my guidance counselor and get a tour. She thinks she is Mother of the Year. As if.

July 8th, 1983

So, TW wants us to go out to dinner tomorrow night and have a heart-to-heart talk. She said she is concerned that I seem angry and, as she puts it, "uncommunicative." She wants me to talk to her about my feelings and tell her exactly how I feel. What am I supposed to say? I hate you because you moved me to Pepto Bismol Gardens in Persnickety? Besides, if she was a real mother she'd know how I feel. She shouldn't have to take me to dinner to find out. A real mother would actually care about how I feel and let me do the things I want to do. She would never have moved me away from Kyle and my real home. She would have been there since I was a baby instead of hanging out with pig people. She would be talking to me about curfews and make sure I didn't get myself into trouble with Kyle. A real mother would be more like Gram. I really miss her. She was strict and I know I should not have gone behind her back, but Gram loves me and I know she misses me as well. She says so every time we talk on the phone. I wish TW could have let me stay in Warwick at least for the summer. When I went back last weekend everybody was talking about stuff going on there and I felt left out. People are talking about eighth grade and Kyle and I don't have as much to talk about either. Most of what we did last weekend was make out. I miss being able to talk to him about stuff. I don't have anything to say because nothing happens here. I hate it here. And I hate TW for bringing me here. I should just tell her I don't want to go out to dinner. She's my mother and I don't even like her.

July 10th, 1983

So I ended up going out for dinner with TW after all. And she went into this whole speech about how she wanted me to open up and discuss my feelings so we could have an open and honest relationship. Really? What a bunch of bullshit. I curse now that nobody can stop me. And I don't care. Gram is the only one who cared. TW wanted me to know that I can say anything to her and that I should feel safe with her. I didn't say anything. I just rolled my eyes and thought is this woman for real? Then she just started talking about herself anyway. She went on and on about how grateful she is for a new start, and how AA changed her life and how her Higher Power is taking care of her and blah, blah, blah. She thinks she is the most interesting person in the world. I just sat there and let her talk. What was I supposed to do? So I ate my food and let her go on and on and… Well, you get the idea.

So she tells me she has this new friend in AA. Her whole life revolves around AA, so I am not surprised. When she is not at work or meetings she is on the phone with those people. She said she has to make three phone calls a day so she doesn't drink or use drugs and so she stays sober and helps other people stay sober. And that is not including all the calls back and forth with her sponsor and now the people she sponsors. I never get to use the phone. It just sucks. The only people I have to talk to are Kyle and Gram and Kyle got in trouble for using the phone to make long distance calls, so he is grounded from the phone. All he can do is write letters. I really wish he would write more. He doesn't really like to write; we thought about sending cassette tapes to each other but what if they get lost in the mail? I don't want some stranger listening to me!

Anyway, so TW wants me to go to the Alateen meeting next Saturday at the library while she is at her AA meeting and then go out to lunch with her friend and her friend's daughter Alicia. I can't believe I have to sit through that stupid meeting for an hour. I hope her friend's daughter is nice. Girls can be very mean. They pretend to be your friend and then behind your back start rumors. I don't trust them. I miss Kyle.

July 18th, 1983

Yesterday was the day I went to the Alateen meeting and then had lunch with TW, Alicia and her mom. First I had to go to the Alateen meeting with Alicia. It was in the library in a separate room from the AA meeting. There were two adults there who were called AMIAS, which means that they are approved as Alateen sponsors. Parents are not supposed to attend and we were told that whatever was said there had to stay there. Speaking was not required but we all had to go around in a circle and say our names. There were about six of us not including the adults. The youngest was a girl by the name of Karen who was 12. The others were teenagers mostly between the ages of 14 to 16. There were mostly girls but a couple of boys. I was given literature which talks about the 12-Steps. It was similar to the stuff TW has lying around the house but talked about how we are not in control of our loved ones who drink. I still don't understand why I had to go. TW does not drink. The other kids were all talking about how their parents' drinking hurt them and how they tried to stop them. I didn't know TW then. When it was my turn, I didn't say anything. What was I supposed to say? I mean Gramps drank but all he did when I saw him was watch TV and fall asleep. How did that hurt me? Gram was always there and she did everything anyway.

When it was Alicia's turn to speak she told about how her mother used to work as a bartender in a bar that had bands in Denville. She lived with her mother and grandmother. She rarely saw her mother on weekends because that is when she worked and her mother would stay after last call to clean up, which was when she would drink and then get home at 4 am and sleep until 3 p.m. Alicia's grandmother had to make her meals and all that stuff. By Monday her mother would be working off a bender and not be able to do much until Wednesday when the next shift started. She said her mother never came to her school events and she could not bring friends home to play because she was embarrassed and usually had to help her grandmother do housework. A lot of times she had to cook for the family, especially if her grandmother, who was sick a lot, didn't feel well. She said she felt lonely and different from other kids. She said she never saw her father, who left when she was a baby and was not part of her life. He lives somewhere in North Carolina now. Her mother finally stopped drinking because she got in a bad car accident coming home from work, driving in a blackout. A blackout is when you drink so much that you don't know what you are doing. I never heard of that before. How do you walk around and not know what you are doing? Is it like sleepwalking? That's creepy. Then her mother got arrested for drunk driving and had to go to AA meetings and now works as a waitress in a diner. The other kids have been going to Alateen for a while, so they all shared about their parents. One kid said his father was a drinker and would go to a bar after work and come home drunk and then get angry, and if there was a toy left out or something would pull them all out of bed and beat him or his brother and then his mom to punish them for making a mess. He said his mother spent all her time making sure the house was spotless and if anyone spilled even a glass of milk at the table she would tell them that Dad was going to come home and beat them with the belt! Sometimes he would beat them for no reason except that he was in a bad mood and had too many bills to pay. He said his father stopped drinking because Family Services got involved, but that things are not much better because now his father is just a dry drunk (whatever that means). But at least the beatings stopped. I had to listen to all of these depressing stories. It made me sad. I've never had any of these experiences. Gram and Gramps were always nice to me and took care of me. Well, Gram did at least. And TW wasn't even around. I barely know her. So, I stayed quiet until the hour was over and we all said the Lord's Prayer. The whole thing just weirded me out. Then it was time for lunch. We went to the diner.

I had grilled cheese and bacon, which is my favorite. TW and Alicia's mom did most of the talking. Of course they wanted to know what I thought of Alateen and if I wanted to join. I tried to be polite because we were in front of other people. What I wanted to say was NO WAY IN HELL. But I didn't, I just said I didn't think so. Later when we went back to Alicia's house, she told me in private that she doesn't like to go either but her mom gives her extra allowance for going. That sounds like bribery to me.

Alicia is a cutter. I never heard of that before. Why would anyone cut themselves on purpose? She told me she's been doing it since she was eight. She showed me scars on her stomach that no one can see because she does it near her private parts. She says it helps make the pain go away when she is upset and that nothing else works. I don't understand that. I think it is grody. How does causing pain stop pain? After we left I told TW I wasn't going back to Alateen and that I didn't like Alicia. She wanted to know why. I wanted to say none of your business but I just said because I don't, that's why. I told her I want to spend weekends with Gram for the rest of the summer. School starts in six weeks, so she said OK I can go every other weekend because it's too much driving for her. So I get to see Gram and Kyle next weekend! I can't wait!

July 20th, 1983

Well I am going back to Gram and Gramps' house this weekend, but not for a good reason. Gramps is in the hospital and it's not good. Gram told TW that he has been swelling up. She called it a funny word something like edema? He has fluid in his stomach and arms and legs and they put him in the ICU in the hospital. I think he might have kidney failure. First his liver went and now his kidneys. Poor Gramps. He is only 63. That is old to me, but still. I feel so bad for Gram. She is beside herself with worry. I'm glad we're going to be with her this weekend. I heard TW telling Gram that it's time to sell the farm. That farm has been in Gramps' family for years; how could TW tell her to do that? That was my home for most of my life. TW just thinks she can march in here and tell everybody what to do. And Gram just takes it. She's always so nice to TW. I know TW is her daughter, but still… I know Gram would say Jesus would forgive her, but I am not Jesus and I won't. Maybe TW will let me stay with Gram for the rest of the summer. I'm going to talk to Gram and see. Plus, if I go back I can see Kyle. Although he has not been writing much. I hope he's not cheating on me with Julia. I feel so sad and mad. Everything in my life has changed and is being taken away from me and I am just supposed to accept it like nothing is wrong. Why is this happening to me?

July 25th, 1983

Gramps is dying. We are spending most of our time at the hospital now. TW took some time off from work so we are staying at Gram and Gramps' house. The doctors said he does not have much time. He was continuing to drink behind Gram's back even after he was diagnosed. I don't know how because she was watching him like a hawk. But he did. Now his organs are shutting down. TW talked Gram into putting the farm on the market. They met with a Realtor who said some housing construction company is interested in buying it and it is worth over $1 million. That's a lot of money for Gram but all I can think about is the farm I love is going to get turned into a housing development. My life as I know it is ending right before my eyes. At least Gramps won't be around to see it. When the farm sells Gram is going to move into our apartment complex and eventually TW wants to buy a house for all of us. None of this seems real to me. How can someone's life change so quickly?

Gramps is still in the ICU and they say it won't be long. He is on dialysis and lots of medication so I can't really talk to him. I brought my guitar with me and played some songs for him. TW spent some time alone with him and when she left she was crying. She did not say what they talked about. Gram has hardly left his side. In fact, I took her to the cafeteria because TW wanted to be alone with him. We only go back to the house to sleep. Gram wanted to stay in the hospital with Gramps, but TW won't let her.

I haven't seen Kyle since I got back. I called him a few times but he wasn't home and he hasn't called me back. Well, to be fair I've been here at the hospital most of the time, but still. I am so sad.

July 29th, 1983

Gramps died today. They disconnected all the tubes. Gram seems like she is in shock. TW is taking care of everything. She called the funeral home and the viewing will be for two days and the funeral the day after. TW has been trying to reach whatever relatives she can. At least she is helping Gram with all of this. I am glad that Gram will be living with us, but I wish it could be at the farm. It seems cruel to take her away from all she has known for years. I know.

August 1st, 1983

The funeral was today. A lot of people from town came to the viewing. Most of the congregation from church came and Gramps' poker buddies. Gram broke down at the burial. We had to hold her back from the grave when they put Gramps in. It was so sad. Everyone was crying. Even TW. Then we came back to the house and the ladies from the church had food for everyone. We now have a ton of casseroles as well. Gram won't have to cook for a while. Kyle actually came to the viewing. He hugged me and told me he was sorry but didn't say much. He didn't even stay or come back to the house after he paid his respects. I feel like I've lost the best friend I ever had. First Gramps and now Kyle. Why won't he talk to me? Julia came with her parents. She told me she was sorry and tried to hug me but I didn't hug her back. I just went up to my old room when everyone left. I've been crying my eyes out. I don't think I have ever felt this much pain in my life. At least I still have Gram. And she will be near me again.

August 8th, 1983

We are heading back to Persnickety tomorrow. TW has to get back to work. Gram is not moving to New Jersey after all. She wants to stay in Warwick where she has lived all her life and has her "church" family. Oh well. Adults always do what they want and it never seems to be what I want. TW promised me we will visit as much as we can, but I know she just wants to stay in NJ on weekends and go to her AA meetings. It does not seem to matter what I want. Besides, there is nothing except Gram for me in Warwick anyway. After all the funeral stuff was done both Gram and TW told me to go to the lake so they could talk and get stuff done. So I did. I tried to call Kyle first to see if he was going but he was already out. Then when I got to the lake I saw them. He was with Julia and they were walking with their arms around each other. I couldn't believe it. How could he do that to me? Then they saw me and Julia ran off to talk to her friends. Kyle came over to me and I'm just standing there like an idiot with my mouth open. He then tells me that he's sorry but I live too far away and he is going out with Julia now. I smacked him in the face and called him an asshole. I know it was wrong and I shouldn't have done it, but how could he humiliate me like that? And to make it worse, Julia and her friends saw the whole thing. I just left after that and walked home. I hate him and I hate her. I hope he knocks her up and she has to go to the pregnant girls high school next year. It would serve that slut right. And Kyle. It's obvious he just wants one thing. I'm done here. In fact, I am done with kids my age, period. I will never trust anyone again.

August 15th, 1983

Well, we're back in Pepto Bismol Gardens. Or at least I am for another three weeks until school starts. TW scheduled an orientation meeting at my new school with my new guidance counselor. She thinks she is such a caring mom. That meeting is next week. TW has to take another day off from work and I guess that's a big sacrifice for her because she has no vacation time left. I have not seen much of her since we got back because all she's been doing is going to work and her AA meetings and that's just fine with me. As long as she doesn't make me go back to that stupid Alateen meeting I don't care what she does. She is making me go out to dinner with her on Saturday nights. She calls it mother/daughter bonding time. More of that stupid shit she learned in EST in California. I finally asked her who my father was. She actually told me she didn't know, that it could be one of a number of people. I was like, how can you possibly not know? Weren't you there at the time? So, she says yes, but it was Woodstock and she doesn't remember much because she was taking LSD (she calls it acid). So basically she is telling me that she was a druggie and a slut at 18. And then ran away and left her baby to boot.

And now I have no idea who my father is or where he is. Why wasn't she on the pill like everybody else? How could she be so stupid? But, I guess if she had been I would not be here.

Right now I don't feel grateful about that. I'm worried about Gram, but she has her church people so she'll be OK. She calls me almost every day and tells me how much she misses me and Gramps. It makes me sad. She wants me to come stay with her on my Thanksgiving break and Christmas break. TW said that's fine. She'll probably be glad to have me out of the house. She thinks I spend all of my time moping around here and feeling sorry for myself. Um, well, whose fault is that? I didn't ask to move here. If she hadn't taken me away Kyle and I would still be together. But now he's with Julia. I hate Kyle and Julia. I don't even want to play guitar anymore because it reminds me of Kyle. I just sit around this dumb apartment watching MTV. I tried going to the pool, but that creepy lifeguard is always there. His name is Eric. He told me he is starting his sophomore year at County College. When I'm there he just stares at me and tries to talk to me even when I have my headphones on listening to my Walkman. Why doesn't he watch the kids like he is supposed to? There is nobody else there my age, either. So, the other day he comes up to me and actually asks me out. I looked at him and told him that my mother wouldn't let me go out with him because I'm only 13. Which is probably true, because I don't think she would. He's like six years older than me! And then he acted all surprised because he thought I was in high school and was 16!

I never really spend much time thinking about what I look like. So I looked in the mirror at myself. I saw a girl with light brown hair with blonde highlights and green eyes. Tan skin, not fat and not skinny, with boobs. Do I really look 16? I don't know. Kyle always said that I was hot, but he was my boyfriend. He was supposed to think that. And besides, if I was that hot why did he cheat on me with Julia? She's not that hot. So she has boobs now. Big whoop. She's so skinny that she looks like a lollipop with boobs on the stick part, especially with her big head. And she thinks she's so hot because she is a cheerleader. Whatever. They can have each other.

August 23rd, 1983

Today was my orientation at Persnickety Middle School. My guidance counselor is Mrs. McFarrell. She looks like a grandmother type. She showed me and TW around the school. As if there was something special about a middle school. It had classrooms, an auditorium, two gyms with locker rooms (one for boys and one for girls), a cafeteria and outside some basketball courts and some playground equipment for the fifth graders. Oh, and lockers. I got my locker and combination and had to practice opening my locker. Like I can't figure out how to open a locker? Really. It looks pretty much like my other school except bigger. Then she sat me down and told me about all the wonderful activities they have and after-school clubs, none of which I am interested in. Like I'm really going to join the Science Club or the Nature Club? Or the Sewing Club? Don't I get enough of that in Home Ec? Oh, and there's a fall and spring eighth-grade play. Mrs. McFarrell wants me to try out since I was in the play in Warwick. This year it's going to be *Charlotte's Web* for the fall and *Carousel* for the spring. TW was all excited and asking me if I thought that sounded great. I wasn't rude to either of them, I just said um, yeah sure. Then TW made a big point of telling Mrs. McFarrell how I was in the Gifted and Talented Program in Warwick and how smart I was and how well I did on the standardized tests. She said she wanted to make sure I was challenged. Like she really knows about my academics. Please. Mrs. McFarrell was all excited and started talking about what a great accelerated program they have for kids like me and that I was just going to love it, blah, blah, blah. Then she wanted to make sure I had my library card so I could do the summer reading assignment. TW never took me to get a card so guess where we went after that? I found the book I have to read and write a report about. It's due September 6th when we go back to school. Guess that is what I'll be doing for the next couple of weeks. Oh, besides Saturday, when TW is going to take me to the Rockaway Mall to do back-to-school shopping. She said I have grown so much that I need all new clothes. What, in the three months she's been back in my life?

I will take new clothes though. I just hope she doesn't make me wear anything dorky. Not that it matters. The kids are probably all snobs anyway. They have known each other since kindergarten. I remember what it was like for new kids when they moved to Warwick. And now here I am, the new kid.

September 6th, 1983

Today was the first day of school. Mrs. McFarrell put me in the smart kids' classes. She also wanted to put me in Band, but I refused. I did sign up for Chorus, but only because we had to choose one or the other as part of our specials classes. We rotate specials after a few months of each. First I have Chorus, then Art, then Home Ec and then Gifted and Talented. So besides getting our lockers (I already had mine) assigned in homeroom, we were supposed to follow our schedules and go to all of our classes, which we did, and got our books. When we had English we handed in our book reports. My lunch is fifth period. Nobody sat with me. In fact, the kids weren't mean or nice. They basically just ignored me and sat with their friends. I sat at the end of a table with the losers who have no friends. We didn't get any homework today so I was able to leave all my books in my locker. TW has to take me to the Kmart in the strip mall near our house to get my supplies. My life is so exciting I can hardly stand it.

September 19th, 1983

I haven't written because I have nothing to say. My life is boring as hell. I go to school, come home, do my homework, which is a lot by the way, and then watch MTV. I haven't played much guitar. I just don't feel like it. Mrs. McFarrell called me down to her office today. I thought I was in trouble because the office buzzed my class and announced for me to come down to Guidance. Of course, everyone stopped what they were doing and stared at me. It was so embarrassing. I couldn't figure out what I did to get in trouble. I hardly speak to anyone! It turned out she just wanted to check on me to see how I am doing and if I feel like I am settling in. I said I am doing OK. Which is true, I am doing OK, I guess. I just don't care about anything. I feel like I am just going through the motions. TW started dating some guy she met in AA. His name is Chris. He's a carpenter or contractor or something. He fixes up houses and then sells them. So now TW is like all obsessed with this guy. They go out every Saturday night. She invited me once and I was like no way in hell. I said I would stay home. Like I really want to go eat dinner with the two of them? I wish I could visit Gram except going back to Warwick would just remind me of Kyle and Julia. Gram could drive to see me except there is no place to stay overnight here and it's a lot of driving for her. She is all involved with her church now anyway. Some construction company made an offer on the farm. They are willing to pay Gram a lot of money. TW told her to take the offer. Gram is thinking about it. I can't believe she is selling the farm. It just doesn't feel real to me.

October 11th, 1983

Mrs. McFarrell called me down again! I am really starting to hate that woman. I should call her TW2. She said she was very happy with my school progress and that my teachers all think I am a very capable bright student, blah, blah, blah, but she is worried that I haven't been making friends. Tryouts for the fall play are this week and she wants me to go. It's that *Charlotte's Web* thing she was talking about. I have nothing to do except go to school and come home, so I said OK.

Gram accepted the offer on the house and she is going to move into a new community just outside of town for active adults. They have all kinds of activities and offer transportation to shopping and church. She's selling the car, too. I thought that I would not get to see her until Thanksgiving, but TW is sending me there this weekend. I think she just wants me out of the house so she can do it with Chris. Whatever. At least I get to see Gram. And we are going back, all three of us, the weekend after to help Gram with her tag sale and packing up the house. I finally agreed to meet Chris. He's OK. He doesn't talk much. He's divorced and has an ex-wife and kid in Virginia. He hardly ever sees his kid. I don't think his ex likes him very much. But TW sure does. Everything is Chris this and Chris that. It makes me want to puke. Well, at least I get out of Pepto Bismol Gardens for a couple of weekends.

October 13th, 1983

Tryouts for *Charlotte's Web* were today after school. I'm not sure how I did. I sang "Day by Day" from *Godspell*. We find out next Monday. Everybody is guaranteed something, even if they don't get a part with lines, there's the chorus and set design. I'm not really artistic so I guess, worst comes to worst, I will just be in the chorus. The play is the first week of December. Then I also have to be in the Christmas chorus concert the week before Christmas because that is part of my grade in that class. I still feel like I'm just going through the motions with all of this. TW2 wants to check in with me once a month to see how I am doing. Doesn't she have anything else to do? It's not like I am the only kid in the school. She called TW1 to get permission and TW1 was all over the idea. She thought it was great. I haven't seen much of her lately because she's either at an AA meeting or out with Chris. She's taking me to Gram's house tomorrow night. It's going to feel weird being back there. I haven't been there since the funeral.

And it's going to be weird knowing that pretty soon the house will be gone and a development will be there instead. All the livestock has been sold. It's going to feel so empty. It's coming to the end of apple season so most of the trees are going to be picked clean. Gram told me she will make me an apple pie. I love her pies. She also said she is going to take me to church with her Sunday morning. TW1 is picking me up Sunday afternoon. At least I won't have to worry about running into Kyle. Julia is another story. I think she still goes to that church. With Gram next to me I have to be on my best behavior but what I would really like to do is El Kabong her with my guitar. At least it would be put to good use.

October 17th, 1983

I didn't get a part in *Charlotte's Web*. The popular kids who have lived in Persnickety all their lives got parts. Big surprise. Adults think they are so caring and nice to kids but they're all just older kids who are hypocrites. Especially TW2. I can't believe I have to go talk to her once a month for the rest of the year. She is so annoying. She's like perpetually cheerful. I'd like to El Kabong her as well as Julia. Put them both in a room and El Kabong away. And yes, I did see Julia when I was at church with Gram, and no I did not El Kabong her. I was Miss Sweetness and Light when she came over to say hello with her parents. She made a point of telling me how sorry she was that things didn't work out for me and Kyle. Like she didn't have anything to do with it? Please. Thankfully, somebody interrupted us to talk to Gram. The whole thing put me in a really bad mood and TW1 was bugging me about it on the car ride home. She kept asking me what was wrong and I kept saying nothing, and she kept saying she wanted me to talk to her and express my feelings. I was ready to El Kabong her too. I think I'd like to El Kabong all three of them, TW1 and TW2 and most of all Julia. But then my guitar would be ruined. I did pick up my guitar when I got home and wrote a song called "I Hate You All." It was acoustic punk. Maybe I should play that at the Christmas concert. Ha! Well, rehearsals start this Thursday after school so I have fewer days to get my homework done, and I have a lot. They're preparing us for high school and we are being prepped for the honors track. It's OK. It gives me something to do besides watch MTV.

October 24th, 1983

I am tired. We spent all weekend helping Gram with her tag sale and getting ready for her move. She has to be out of the house by November 1st. The movers are coming on Halloween. Trick or treat. It was really sad seeing some of the stuff that I grew up with get sold. Off to new homes and it will probably never be loved as much as it was with us. I just went up to my old bedroom and cried. It feels like everything is being taken away. Gram doesn't even seem to mind. It's really weird. It seems like she is almost happy to be starting a new life. I heard her telling TW1 she feels like a weight has been lifted from her and that she hasn't felt this free in years. In fact, she is planning a month-long cruise in January. Why is it that I am the only one feeling sad these days? Gram also really likes Chris. She thinks he's a "nice, fine fellow" and that he's good for TW1. Even though they are doing it. I know she knows, she just pretends she doesn't. I just hope TW1 doesn't do it with him when I am there. That's all I need. Instead of one idiot downstairs howling like a train now I will have three. Gross. Oh well. Time to get my homework done.

November 3rd, 1983

Gram is in her new condo. She says she loves it. I haven't seen it yet, but I will. Get this, I will be spending Thanksgiving alone with Gram. TW1 and Chris are spending it with his family. Apparently he has a pretty big family. They all live somewhere in Sussex Country, NJ. Pretty much the whole lot of them. Chris grew up on a farm, too, in some place called Wantage. He has like five brothers and sisters and they all have kids and his parents still live on their farm. I'm not unhappy though. I like the idea of spending Thanksgiving alone with Gram. She's going to let me help cook dinner and make pies. I love her pie; oh, I think I already said that before. She has a guest room just for me. It has my old bed and dresser. It will be really weird to see them in a new place. She also told me more about her cruise. She decided it's time for her to see the world. She's going to Spain, France, Italy, Greece, Turkey and Israel. She wants to see the religious sites in Jerusalem. Sounds good to me. A lot better than being stuck in Persnickety in the middle of winter. Gram seems like she's having the time of her life. She joined all of these clubs where she lives, in addition to her church stuff. And she started swimming because they have an indoor/outdoor pool. She says I'll love it. I don't know. It doesn't feel right to me. It doesn't even seem like she misses Gramps. Next thing I know she'll have a boyfriend. I'm sorry but the world is a weird place. Everything is upside down to me and nobody seems to care. Except TW2, who is annoying as hell.

November 15th, 1983

I have been pretty busy lately. Lots of homework and rehearsals. I hardly ever see TW1. I just get up and go to school and come home. There is a late bus on the days I have rehearsal so she doesn't have to worry about how I get home. She's either at AA meetings or with Chris. I kind of like having the apartment to myself. I want to get a cat because we're allowed to have cats (not dogs), but TW1 doesn't want a litter box in the house and we can't let a cat outside because it could get run over. I've been trying to wear her down (when I actually see her) and she finally said we'll see. I'm the one who'll be changing the litter anyway; it's not like she is ever here. I am becoming a pretty good cook. I can make spaghetti and meatballs, and I tried making a stir fry the other day. TW1 lets me order pizza a lot or Chinese. But that gets boring after a while. She only cooks on Sunday. And we have dinner with Chris. She tries to make stuff that will have leftovers for me. Because she is such a caring mother.

November 30th, 1983

Well, Thanksgiving came and went. It was nice to see Gram and I enjoyed cooking with her. But I am sick of turkey and Thanksgiving leftovers. Well, except for pie. She introduced me to some of her new friends. They were nice I guess, for old people. I went swimming with her in the pool at the clubhouse. It was me, Gram and a bunch of old people and some little kids who were visiting their grandparents. Gram's condo is nice I guess. It's not very big, but she says it is just the right size for her and she doesn't even have to clean it. They provide maid service in her community. She doesn't cook much anymore either, because she says it's not fun to just cook for herself. They serve dinner every night at the clubhouse, so she goes there a lot and eats with her friends. We had dinner there Saturday night. It wasn't bad. I think she's a better cook than they are, but whatever.

But here's the kicker. TW1 and Chris got engaged! They couldn't wait to tell me when they came to pick me up. TW1 has this giant rock on her finger and she was just glowing. Good for them. I mean Chris is OK and all but it seems kind of fast to me. Oh, and then it gets better. They put an offer on a house together! They are going to fix it up and we are all going to move there in the summer after they get married and go on their honeymoon. So I get to move again. That's fine. I'll be glad to get out of Pepto Bismol gardens. The house is in someplace called Hackettstown near a college. They're going to start working on it in January. So they'll be spending a lot of time there on weekends and TW1 will have to give up her precious AA meetings on Saturdays and Sundays. She is all about getting married now so she doesn't care. The play is coming up soon and so is the chorus concert. Let's see if she remembers the dates and actually comes to see them.

December 15th, 1983

Well, TW1 missed both the play and the concert. Gram doesn't have a car anymore, so she didn't come either. It doesn't matter. They were both lame anyway. I'm not going to do the spring play, but I have to do the spring chorus concert because it's part of my grade. Christmas break is coming up soon and I'll be glad to get away from that school for a while. TW2 called me down for my monthly meeting with her. I told her that TW1 was getting married in June and that I would be moving. She got all upset. I told her I wasn't upset. I don't know why she is. I don't want to be in this town anyway. I don't have any friends here and I don't like the kids. I wish I could move now. TW1 and Chris took me to Hackettstown where the house is. We couldn't go in because they don't own it yet. It's what they call a Victorian. It looks like a lot of the houses in Warwick and the town is much more like where I used to live. It has a downtown with a record store and movie theater and stores and some bars and restaurants. The house is near the college so that's kind of cool. Plus, I can walk almost anywhere. I'll be glad to live in a town that's not one big strip mall and office park.

1984

January 7th, 1984

So the holidays came and went. I spent Christmas and New Years with Gram. TW1 and Chris went to Cancun for a romantic getaway. Good for them. TW1 is still all glowy about getting married. They're going to have the ceremony at this country inn in Hackettstown and she is having a Victorian wedding dress designed for her by a bridal shop that's also in Hackettstown. She found some AA meetings there so starting this month she is going to go to one on Saturdays there and then help Chris work on the house when he is in between projects. So, I'll be spending a lot of my time in Pepto Bismol land by myself. Whatever.

Anyway, it was nice to spend time with Gram for Christmas. She made all my favorite Christmas food and cookies, but it was weird being in her new townhouse. Her present to me was to take me shopping for clothes and music tapes at the mall. She said it was from her, TW1 and Chris combined, but I think TW1 was just too lazy to get me a present. Gram and I picked out TW1's present together and got her a necklace to wear at the wedding. I gave it to her when she got back from Cancun and she said she loved it. I gave Gram a framed picture of the old house and it made her cry, but she said she loved it too, so I guess I did well.

I spent New Year's Eve with the old people where Gram lives and their grandchildren. They had a buffet dinner in the clubhouse and then dancing with old people music after. Then they televised the ball dropping in Times Square. They gave all the kids sparkling cider for the toast instead of champagne. It was pretty lame, but hey, it was a bunch of old people. I wonder if Kyle was with Julia at the first night celebration in town. I'm kind of glad I didn't have to see that, even if I did get stuck with a bunch of old people.

So now it's back to school and I have a lot of work, so

that is going to keep me busy. We have to prepare for the eighth grade state tests in March in addition to our regular work, so we have a ton more homework. I don't care. I don't have anything else to do except listen to my tapes or watch MTV. Sometimes I pull out the guitar, but I don't write songs anymore. TW2 called me down to talk to me about high school. I reminded her I was moving but she said that I was an honor student and wanted to make sure that I was scheduled for honors classes in high school next year. She said she was going to contact the Hackettstown High School guidance department to talk to them. I can't pick electives until I am registered there. TW1 probably won't register me until sometime in the summer after her honeymoon so I'll probably get all the lame electives. Well, I guess that's about it. TW1 and Chris are going to take me with them to the house next Saturday. I have a bunch of homework to do so I'll probably just walk to the library in town and do it there while they do whatever it is they do. Then we're going out to a restaurant in town and back to the apartment for the night, and they go back to work on the house on Sunday. My life is so exciting I can't stand it.

March 17th, 1984

I have not written in months because I have nothing to say. My life has been pretty much the same. I go to school, do my homework, watch MTV and visit Gram for a weekend once a month. Except for January because she was on a cruise. TW1 and Chris work on the house on the weekends and go to their AA meetings. They bring me with them on Saturdays so I either walk around Hackettstown or go to the library. They don't have cable in the house, obviously, so I can't watch MTV. I visited the record store in town. It has a pretty good selection but not for cassette tapes. I wish I had a stereo. Maybe I'll ask TW1 for one for my birthday. State tests are next week and then I'll be spending spring break and Easter with Gram. She's going to take me to the mall for spring and summer clothes because TW1 doesn't have time. When she's not working, at her meetings or at the new house, she's planning her wedding. Most of the people that are coming are AA people. She's not having any alcohol at the wedding. Too bad, watching adults get drunk and stupid can be very entertaining. I am going to be a bridesmaid and I have to wear a stupid pink dress. I hate it. The other bridesmaids and maid of honor are all AA people and adults. I'm going to be the only teenager there. And the band is going to play all sixties music. Ugh. Not that she was going to hire Tears for Fears anyway.

April 17th, 1984

So get this … Julia really is pregnant!! I found out when I went to church with Gram for Easter and she wasn't there and it was the big, juicy gossip with all the other kids. Serves her right, and Kyle too, except his life won't change much. She's not going to school anymore and is getting home instruction for the rest of the year. Then she has to go to the pregnant girls high school. I know I should be more compassionate and feel bad for her, but I don't. And if I have sex with someone (not that there are any guys I want to do that with) I will make sure I use birth control. I don't want my life getting ruined. I don't even know if I want kids. Maybe someday, but not now! I don't want a life like TW1 either. I want to go to college and have a career and a life. Anyway, I have two months until the school year is over and TW1 wants me to stay with Gram for the first part of the summer when she is on her honeymoon. She wants me to move into the house in August.

May 19th, 1984

Well, my birthday came and went. I'm 14 now. Old enough to get working papers but since I'll be spending one month in NY with Gram and then moving into the new house it's going to be impossible for me to get a job. I was thinking maybe the concession stand at the lake near Gram's, but she doesn't drive, it's all the way across town and too far to walk. I don't have a bicycle at her townhouse and they want people for all summer because the lake doesn't close until Labor Day. So I guess I can go there and hang out with the old people. Anyway, we had my birthday celebration in Warwick since Gram doesn't have a car anymore. I got a joint birthday present from TW1, Chris and Gram – a stereo! I was really surprised and happy. Now I need to get some records. I'm looking forward to browsing in the record store when I'm in Hackettstown. They have a movie theater across from the record store too, so when I'm there on Saturdays I can go to the movies. I heard there's a new movie coming out called *Sixteen Candles* and it sounds good. I want to see it but I don't have anyone to go with and going by myself is kind of lame. But I guess it's better than sitting in the library. The house is just about done except for some inside painting and I'll be helping with that. I get to choose the color for my room. I picked purple and black. TW1 and Chris were not thrilled, but they said OK. I told them I would paint it myself. I guess it is the least I can do. The wedding is coming soon and I've been going for fittings for the bridesmaid dress. One of TW1's AA friends is having a shower for her and I'm invited. I guess I have to go. I'll ask Gram what to get her. I wish I had a job and some of my own money and didn't have to ask for money all the time. But TW1 wants me to wait until next summer unless I want to babysit. There's a class at the hospital in Hackettstown I can take and get a piece of paper that says I'm a certified sitter, but it meets on Tuesdays at 4 p.m. and I have no way to get there right now. I feel like I'm just sitting tight waiting for something to happen. I can't wait to get out of Pepto Bismol Gardens and that'll happen soon. TW1 wants us out of the apartment by June 1st when the lease is up, but I have school so she had to get the landlord to agree to extend the lease by a month. We have to have all of our stuff packed up before the wedding and then as soon as school is out I go to Gram's house. I can't wait. I hate Persnickety and I will be glad to get out of that middle school and not have to meet with TW2 anymore. I have one monthly meeting left, thank God.

June 30th, 1984

So TW1 got married last Saturday and we have moved out of Pepto Bismol Gardens and I never have to go to school in Persnickety again! Yay!! And of course, TW2 called me down for my last visit the last week of school and was her usual annoying self. I am glad I'm done with that! And I'm looking forward to starting my new life in Hackettstown. But for now, I'm with Gram. I love Gram, I really do, but it is really boring here. There's nobody my age, just old people and their grand-children, who mostly are young kids. The parents pawn them off on the grandparents so they don't have to hire babysit-ters during the summer. So when I go to the pool, it is all these screaming kids. I just put on my Walkman. But that gets boring too, and Gram doesn't really like to go out all that much, especially because her community has a clubhouse and restaurant. She spends a lot of time there playing cards and bingo and hanging out with the other old people. Oh, so I almost forgot. The wedding finally happened, like I said. I never have to wear that stupid bridesmaid dress again. But it was OK. TW (I am back to calling her TW because there is no more TW2) looked very pretty and Chris looked handsome and her boss gave her away and made a toast about being a stand-in dad, which made everyone cry. Well, everyone except TW. I think she still hates Gramps. I wish I knew why but she never talks about him. So, back to the wedding. Every-thing went smoothly because nobody got drunk. We had lots of pictures taken and everyone said we all looked beautiful. Then TW and Chris took off in a limo to go to a hotel and then Bermuda for two weeks. Then they come home and have a couple of weeks alone in the house before I move in. I'm glad it's over. So much planning and wedding talk and blah, blah,

blah. *Sixteen Candles* hasn't come to Hackettstown yet, but hopefully it will be showing when I get there in late July. Oh well, guess I'll go to the pool and listen to my Walkman and read because there is nothing else to do around here.

July 24th, 1984

I am in my new house and my room looks great! It is so nice to be living in a house where my bedroom is not over the train man and I can walk into town and do stuff without having to be driven anywhere. I finally got to see *Sixteen Candles*. I loved it! Molly Ringwald is a really good actress and Anthony Michael Hall was the perfect geeky guy. Except he was really funny, in a good way I mean. I wouldn't tell anyone this but I kind of liked him better than that Jake guy. I mean, yeah, he was really good looking and I was glad she got him in the end, but he just seemed kind of boring to me. And her sister. Ugh. I need to get some friends. It's kind of lame that I am talking like this about a movie. But I have a hard time talking to kids I don't know. I saw this girl in the record store when I was looking at albums. She seemed so confident. She's a punk girl with pink hair, and has a safety pin in her ear. But she is one of those naturally pretty girls who probably could have been a total prep. I don't know her name, but she looks like she's about my age. Maybe I'll get the nerve to ask her. I think she told the owner she lives in Panther Valley. That's a community nearby that has a gate and a clubhouse, pool and golf course. Kind of like Gram's except it's single-family homes and townhomes and is much bigger. Oh, and has families, not just old people. I guess I'll meet people when I start school. The high school is right behind the town pool, which I've been to a few times. It's OK. A lot of kids go there, but I'm afraid to talk to them. I saw some of them looking at me. They must know I'm new. Hackettstown High School is a regional school so kids from Allamuchy (where Panther Valley is) and Liberty and Independence go there, but not all of these kids go to the town pool. Mostly it's people who live in town. There was one guy I saw who looked cute, but I think he has a girlfriend. So when I go I just listen to my Walkman and read books. Now that my stereo is set up I can listen to albums. I just got the sound track to *Sixteen Candles*. I also like Wang Chung's song "Dance Hall Days" so I got that album, too. My stereo has a radio as part of the receiver but the station I like doesn't come in well. The only station I get is from the college in town and they play some pretty weird stuff. I wonder what it's like to work at a radio station. I bet it is kind of cool. Even if it is just a college station. I wish the high school had one. I have to go register soon and pick electives. TW brought home a booklet about the courses. I'm in all honors classes for academics. I have summer reading for English. I have to read *To Kill A Mockingbird* and write a report on it. I can't decide which electives I want. They only have Symphonic Band (no guitar), which I am not interested in, and a Cooking class, a Sewing class, Art, Woodshop and Chorus. I guess I'll just see what's available. I have to go to orientation at the end of August. Then I'll meet the ninth grade guidance counselor (I hope she is not like TW2!) and the other new kids. Everyone else had their orientation last May. I hope the kids are nice. I really do. I hated the kids in Persnickety.

August 15th, 1984

School starts in two weeks. Orientation for me is August 30th. I have to meet with my guidance counselor. It's a woman whose name is Mrs. Swiskey. Sounds like whiskey. Anyway, I hope she isn't a pain in the ass like the last one. *Purple Rain,* the movie, is coming to the Hackettstown Theater this weekend. I can't wait to go, I love Prince! I saw the ads for it on TV. It looks really good. Of course, since I don't know anybody yet I have to go by myself, but I'm getting used to that. I have some allowance money I got for doing chores around the house so I'm going to get the soundtrack album as well. I am starting to build up an album collection but without a lot of money it's going very slowly. I've been going to the pool a lot. Some kids are starting to say hi, but I haven't met anyone I really want to get to know except for the girl with pink hair and she never goes to the pool. I've seen her a couple of times in the record store and said hi and she said hi back, but that's about it. I think her name is Joni. The guy behind the counter who takes special orders asked for it. She gets all these albums by bands I have never heard of. I think she used to live in NYC so she knows a lot about music. I hope I have some classes with her. Other than that, I did see the cute guy at the pool, but he definitely has a girlfriend and she seems like one of the popular kids and a bitch.

August 31st, 1984

So I met with Mrs. Swiskey this morning. She was OK. She went over my schedule with me and helped me pick out electives. I'm in Chorus and Art. She will only be my guidance counselor for ninth grade. She has all the ninth graders and then the other three guidance counselors split up grades 10-12. Ninth graders have to eat lunch in the cafeteria, but tenth and eleventh graders get to eat anywhere on school grounds and seniors get to leave campus for lunch. I'm in all honors classes, no surprise. She also really wants me to join an after-school or lunch club. None of them looked interesting to me except Poetry Club, which is a lunch club. I may join that. I don't really want to be eating in the cafeteria with a bunch of kids I don't know. I hated that last year. TW took me to the mall and got me back-to-school clothes. And I got a haircut at the salon in town. I don't know if I like it or not. I mean I guess it looks OK, I don't look like a dork or anything, but I wish I could get a punk haircut like that girl Joni. TW and Chris are taking me to the shore for Labor Day weekend and then school starts. Not much else going on right now. Except I have to finish my book report for English. I don't want to do it at the shore!

September 4th, 1984

So school started and it is not bad at all. And Joni is in my classes! We hang out at lunch together. She's new as well. She moved here from NYC with her mother this summer and hates it. Her father still lives in the city and she goes to his apartment on the weekends. He's Jewish and lives on the Upper West Side. I don't know a lot of Jewish people. We didn't really have any in Warwick. There were some in Persnickety but they never talked to me. Joni doesn't go to temple though because her mother isn't Jewish. Her mom is a marketing executive in New York and works long hours, so Joni is by herself a lot during the week. She's really into music, especially punk and indie (whatever that is). She likes bands like The Lyres and The Clash. I have never heard of them, but she said I can come over after school and she'll play the albums for me. She's the only one in our grade with pink hair. The other kids think she's weird and stay away from her, especially the Allamuchy kids who take the bus to school and are all preps. And she said her father is really cool and that I can come stay over when she visits him on weekends. She likes to hang out in the Village and go shopping and go to a used record store there. She really wants to go to CBGB but needs a fake ID. I think she looks older than she is but she says they'll card her. I think it would be cool to go to a punk club. I hope TW lets me go with her to her Dad's some weekend. Oh, and she joined the Poetry Club so I did, too. There's not a lot of kids in it, but there are a few and some boys; it's not just girls. They seem nice and the teacher who runs it is my English teacher. He is really cool. He's from California. I wonder how he ended up in Hackettstown? His name is Mr. Stone and he's in his 20s. Half the girls in our class have a crush on him. Because I'm in honors we get a lot of work, and especially a lot of homework. The rest of my classes are OK. Since most of them are honors classes a lot of the kids are from the richer families so they talk about doing stuff I don't get to do much of. Like horseback riding lessons and ski trips and, of course, going to the mall. So I'm glad I met Joni. The boys are kind of dorky, but Joni says boys mature slower than girls and that the best boys are upperclassmen. They keep us freshman pretty separate except for clubs, so it's kind of hard to get to know them. Although the boys in Poetry Club are upperclassmen. They seem kind of cool. And some of them drive, so if we hang out with them we get to get out of town. It's already better than Persnickety. I'm going to visit Gram this weekend, but I'm going to see if I can go with Joni to her dad's next weekend. TW wants to meet Joni first and talk to her dad. Whatever. She has to act like a parent, I get it. But I know she loves having me out of the house on weekends. Living with her and Chris is OK. If I help out around the house they leave me alone.

September 30th, 1984

So, TW finally met Joni and her mom. We went to Joni's townhouse in Panther Valley. And she liked them, but she thinks Joni looks kind of peculiar. She's OK with it though because Joni is an honor student. She and Joni's mom hit it off right away, they sat down with some coffee and were chattering away. Joni and I hung out in her room and listened to The Clash. They are cool. Joni says they're from England but they come to the U.S. and play at CBGB. I wish I was older so I could go. Anyway, since TW met Joni and her mom and likes them I get to go with Joni to her dad's apartment for Columbus Day weekend, which is a three day weekend. TW and Chris are going to go somewhere romantic in the Poconos. They have hotels with private heart-shaped bathtubs. I've seen the commercials on TV. Thank God I don't have to go with them. I can't wait to get to NYC. I never get to go there because Chris and TW don't really like to go to the city. Joni's dad lives near the Museum of Natural History and I have always wanted to go there again ever since I went on a class trip when I was in third grade. That feels like so long ago. I never got to go to the planetarium because that was not included in the admission fee and costs extra. TW is being nice and giving me money to take with me to go to the museum and do other stuff. I'm also going to earn some extra money by doing chores so I can go to the Village with Joni and see her favorite used record store and favorite clothing stores. She has the best clothes! I would like to get my ear pierced and get multiple piercings. There's a place Joni went to that will do it, but I don't want to push my luck with TW. Maybe the next time I go. At least I hope there is a next time! So, Poetry Club is not bad. It meets once a week. There is a senior guy in it I really like but I am too afraid to talk to him. He always compliments my poems though. He found out I play guitar and told me I should put my poems to music. I was afraid to tell him I've done that. Mr. Stone would tell me to bring in my guitar and perform for everyone and I think I'd be too embarrassed in front of the senior guy. He has a name, it's Tyler. He lives in Hackettstown as well. I secretly followed him home from school and he lives in a really nice house right across from the college. I think his father is a lawyer in town. But as soon as I saw him go in his house I left. If he saw me following him that would be like the worst thing ever! I told Joni I like him and she thinks he's cute, too, but she likes this other guy in the club who is a Junior and lives in Panther Valley. His name is Jason, but he has a girlfriend who lives in another town. Joni is hoping that they break up and he will ask her out. I don't know if that's realistic; all of his poems are about his girlfriend and it seems like he really loves her. I think Joni should find someone else, but she said most of the guys at our school are lame and boring and the smart ones are all preps. She likes Jason because she thinks he has a brain and a soul and he's not just a dumb jock.

Hackettstown High School has a lot of different cliques. There are the jocks, student council kids, the stoner heavy-metal freaks, the stoner deadheads, the nerds and the preps/

popular kids. Joni and I just kind of keep to ourselves. Personally, I hate heavy metal and the Grateful Dead and I think pot is a hippie drug. Joni and I are the only ones who like punk music. I've started to listen to punk now. I went to the record store in town and got some Clash records and the Sex Pistols album. I don't really watch MTV anymore now that I have a stereo. There's a punk show on the college station but it's only on once a week, on Monday nights at 10. If I keep the sound low I can listen on my stereo, but I have to be careful because Chris hates punk music and if he hears it he tells me to turn that shit off. Yeah, he says it like that. Chris has a temper, I found out. He hasn't hit me or anything, but he can be pretty mean when he's mad. He's pretty strict too. He won't take any back talk and he expects me to keep my room clean and picked up and he wants me to clean the house on Saturdays so that TW gets a break. At least I get an allowance for that. TW says that he used to be much worse when he was drinking. I guess she heard stories at her AA meetings when he shared. I know he's sorry that he never sees his kid. But if this is what he is like sober then I can only imagine what he was like when he was drinking.

October 10th, 1984

So I got to go to Joni's dad's apartment and stay in NYC over the weekend. It was so cool! Friday night her dad took us for dinner and then Joni and I went to the planetarium to see the laser rock show. It was pretty cool, but not really the kind of music I listen to. On Saturday, Joni took me down to the Village and showed me all the cool stores on 8th street she likes and we went to the used record store and I picked up some albums for my collection. I found some used Television albums. I like them a lot. And some Patti Smith. Anyway, I bought this really cool skirt that is sort of like a combination of shorts and a skirt and I wore it to school Tuesday. I got a lot of compliments, even from the preppy kids. Joni showed me the place where she got her hair done. They'll dye it for you but it's cheaper to do it yourself. I think I would just have them do it because I wouldn't want to mess up the color and have to cut my hair off! So, I have to save up some money to get that done the next time I go back. Joni also showed me where to get my ears pierced. I have to save up for that, too. But they don't check ID so I'm good there. Speaking of ID, since we don't have any we couldn't get into any clubs. Joni said she heard about this place in Times Square that does fake IDs for $10, so I think we're going to try to go there, too. I love New York! It's so much more interesting than Hackettstown. Plus, there's a bus from H'town that goes into the city so it's really easy to get there. Joni's dad is pretty cool. He basically lets us do whatever we want. He spends most of his time with his girlfriend anyway. I can't wait until I can go back. Joni's home this weekend so I think we're just going to hang out in H'town and maybe go to the movies. Tyler got a job at the record store so we're going to visit him. He gets off of work at 6 p.m. so we may hang out with him. Jason's still got a girlfriend, but Tyler said they got in a big fight last weekend and may be breaking up, so Joni is all psyched. There is a spot in the woods where those guys meet up to make campfires. We can bring a boombox and listen to tapes, so we'll probably check that out. Well, that's about it. Time to do homework.

October 29th, 1984

So, Tyler had a Halloween party at his house on Saturday night since Halloween is on a weekday this year. It was wild. His parents weren't home and they got a keg and people got really wasted. Jason was there and he did break up with his girlfriend, so now Joni is going out with him and the four of us have been hanging out together. I can't believe I am dating a senior! I haven't told TW yet because we haven't gone out alone yet, but it's coming. I hope she's cool about it. Maybe if we just say we're going to one of the football games on Friday night and as long as I am back home at 11 for curfew she won't care. Chris is the one I'm more worried about. He thinks he's my father and can tell me what to do all the time. TW just lets him do that. It really pisses me off. He's not my father and never will be. And if he finds out I drink I am really in trouble. But I got away with it this weekend because I stayed at Joni's house and her mom is always out. Joni wants us to all go to the city after we get our IDs. The guys need them too because the drinking age just went up, although none of us are 18 anyway, duh. I can't wait until we get back to the city. It looks like I can go with Joni next weekend and the guys can meet us there. Anything to get out of my house. I can't stand being around TW and Chris.

November 9th, 1984

We got our IDs! It was really easy. We just went to this place near Times Square, handed over our money and they made them. I am now a junior at SUNY Oswego. So, the guys met us in the city on Saturday night and during the day I got my hair cut in a punk cut and got it dyed blue! It is so awesome. I also got seven piercings in my left ear. I thought it was going to hurt, but it didn't. I have to make sure the holes don't get infected and have to keep the studs in for a month before I take them out so the holes don't close up. The four of us tried to get into CBGB to see a band but the line was too long and when we got to the door the show was sold out. So we ended up going to this random bar in the Village and we didn't even get carded. Then we went to Washington Square Park to hang out. We wanted to go back to Joni's but her dad was there. The guys had to leave by midnight to catch the last bus. Then when I got home Sunday TW was all pissed about my hair and getting my ears pierced and Chris told her to ground me. Which she did. So now I'm stuck at home for the next two weekends. Thanksgiving is coming up and TW is sending me to Gram's. I love Gram and all but it is really boring at her townhouse and there's nothing for me to do. I'm trying to see if I can come home that Friday, except I won't have a ride. TW and Chris are going to stay with his family. I was invited but I didn't want to go, so they said I should go to Gram's and they didn't want either me or Gram to be alone so there you go. My life is going to be pretty boring for the next couple of weeks. I can hang out with my friends after school but have to be home by six. Really? But, I get to spend my winter break with Joni at her dad's and I get to be there from the day after Christmas to New Year's.

November 15, 1984

So I'm on house arrest (that's what I call grounding) for another week. Tyler's going to be working a lot more hours at the record store for the holiday season and keeping holiday hours so we aren't going to get to spend a lot of time together outside of school. I haven't told TW and Chris about him yet. One thing at a time. Joni is going to stay over this weekend to keep me company, and then next weekend is Thanksgiving so she'll be at her Dad's and I'll be with Gram. I was hoping that Gram would let us cook a turkey and I was going to make us dinner, but she wants to eat at the clubhouse with me and the old people. She doesn't seem to want to cook much anymore now that she doesn't have to. I told her I would do it but no, she wants to be with her friends, so I'll have to make polite chit-chat with old people all weekend. All they ask me about is school and there isn't much to say about that. Gram tells them I am an honor student and blah, blah, blah, so they ask me about that. And then they go back to talking about their grandchildren, and their aches and pains and blah, blah, blah. Getting old seems really boring. They have movie night in the clubhouse Friday night and a singer with a sing-along Saturday night. Whoop de doo. I wish Gram could just visit me for the day on Thanksgiving. I would cook us a real Thanksgiving dinner. And make pie. If she would give me her recipe. Well, anyway, not much else going on except that report cards came out and I got grades of 90 and above so that made TW and Chris happy, and maybe now I can tell them about Tyler. He wants to take me to the movies the Friday after Thanksgiving because he has the night off. So I have to behave to make sure I can go. At least he doesn't have blue hair or ear piercings so that will help!

November 30th, 1984

Well, Thanksgiving came and went. It was pretty much what I expected, but it was good to see Gram. She seems happy with her friends. Although she has been getting a lot of what she calls heartburn. I asked her if she went to see a doctor but she says it's just from eating too much good food. TW and Chris are going to bring her here for Christmas Eve and day. I'm glad we're having Christmas here this year. I am actually looking forward to getting the tree this weekend and decorating. Oh, and TW and Chris said yes about Tyler and they like that he lives in town and that his father is a lawyer. Thank God. So I get to go to the movies with him tonight. We're going to see *Gremlins*. It finally came to H'town. He's going to come with us to get our tree at Berk's farm and have dinner with us Saturday. Joni's going to be at her dad's but the four of us are going to try to do something next weekend. I am actually in a pretty good mood; maybe it's the holiday spirit. Chris has been in a good mood which helps. He's not yelling so much these days. So I'm trying not to rock the boat. I haven't done my Christmas shopping yet, but I still have time. I think I might get TW and Chris a gift certificate to a restaurant in town, Gram a bracelet I think she'd like, and Joni an album she wants. I'm not sure what to get Tyler and I should get Jason something, but I have no idea what to get him. Maybe I'll get Tyler a winter scarf. No, that sounds lame. It's so hard to know what guys like. It's not like I can get him a case of Heineken. I know he'd like that! Oh, and sex. I know he wants to do it but I don't think I'm ready yet. I haven't had to deal with that lately because we don't have a lot of chances to be alone. Plus, it's too cold to visit our spot in the woods. TW tried to have "the talk" with me. She's worried because he is older and a senior. I told her not to worry, I am still a virgin and have no desire to get pregnant and end up like Julia. But I don't think Tyler will wait forever. Joni says she knows a free clinic where we can get on the pill, but then I would feel like a slut. If he knows I'm on the pill, then that's basically like saying go ahead. I'm not going to worry about it until we've been dating for six months. That's when everyone thinks you're doing it anyway.

December 7th, 1984

Christmas is getting closer. We got our tree and Tyler helped us decorate, and to win brownie points he also helped me make Christmas cookies to give as presents. TW and Chris still like him so I'm keeping my fingers crossed. They don't know he and I drink together sometimes. But since it's still the Christmas season he's working a lot, so we don't get a lot of alone time, especially because my curfew is at 11 p.m. Joni's dad is letting her have all of us at his apartment on New Year's Eve and he's going out, so it will be awesome! I can't wait! Tyler's friends with one of the DJs at the college station so he's going to be getting a show starting in January on Friday nights from 8-11 p.m., so we can hang out there together! He's going to let me pick some of the music for his shows. I think being on the radio will be really cool! So, as you can see I'm in a pretty good mood lately. Life is good.

1985

January 2nd, 1985

I got back home this morning. School starts tomorrow. I was so hungover on New Year's Day I could barely move. TW and Chris wanted me to come home yesterday but I told them I had a stomach virus, which by some miracle they believed. I still felt pretty lousy today but they let me alone to take a nap as long as I promised to do homework before I went to bed. Staying at Joni's was awesome!! We didn't get into CBGB but we found this other club that was really cool. There was a DJ playing punk music and we stayed out until 4 a.m. and drank and Joni's dad didn't even know. She doesn't have a curfew as long as she calls to check in and let him know she's OK. How awesome is that?? We spent a lot of time in the Village and down by Washington Square Park and NYU. I bet it's really cool to be a student there. You get to live right in the city! I was going to get some more piercings but I decided not to because I don't want to get grounded from Tyler, especially now that he's starting his radio show. I'll get to hang out with him alone every Friday night (except when Joni and Jason are there), but Tyler and I can fool around if nobody else is there and he puts a long song on. He's getting into some interesting music lately. He likes The Lyres, Rain Parade and The Green Pajamas. I had never heard of them but he played some for us when we were at Joni's dad's apartment and they're pretty cool. I was able to find a Lyres album at the used record store in the Village, but Chris will never let me play it in the house when he's there. He's all about country music. Eww. So anyway, New Year's Eve was amazing! The guys took the bus into the city and Joni's dad was out all night on a date so we had the whole apartment to ourselves. The guys brought a case of beer (not Heineken, too expensive). It was Bud but better than nothing and we all got really whacked. Joni and Jason went into her room for most of the night, and Tyler and I were in the living room. We listened to records and made out and started fooling around, and I was feeling really good and then he wanted to do it. I was tempted, but I'm not on the pill and he didn't have a condom. He was pretty frustrated with me but then he got in a better mood when I told him I could give him a blow job. He really seemed to like that so I think I'm safe for a while now. Although personally, I think it's kind of gross. I had to run out and brush my teeth afterwards, but he told me he loved me and was really sweet to me the rest of the night. The guys couldn't stay because Joni's dad was coming home sometime after midnight. They had to take all the empty beer cans with them too and dump them in the trash so we wouldn't get in trouble. They almost missed the last bus back to H'town, but somehow they made it. And then since Joni and I felt like shit the next day (New Year's Day) we had to tell her dad we had food poisoning, which he believed. I had to remember to keep my stories straight because I told TW I had a stomach bug, but she wasn't really prying so it was cool. Anyway, tomorrow it's back to school and then Friday I get to spend the afternoon with Tyler and then go up to the radio station. He's back to working only on Saturday days, so we have more time together. So far 1985 is off to a great start!

January 20th, 1985

January has been pretty good. TW and Chris are leaving me alone, especially because I shovel snow for them without being asked. I've been spending Friday nights with Tyler at the station. Sometimes Joni and Jason come up too. Tyler's been teaching me how to cue records and may let me guest-host. He is so creative. I don't know if I could think up enough stuff to play for three hours. The studio has a record library with some decent stuff and the student station manager (I haven't met her yet) gets CDs from record companies so I've gotten to check out some new stuff. Tyler really likes the obscure, trippy psychedelic bands as opposed to straight punk bands. He likes to smoke pot up there, too – to me I'd rather just stick to booze. Pot just makes me think of hippies and TW. I don't want to be her. But booze kind of knocks off the rough edges just enough so that I can laugh and have a good time, and I feel much more relaxed when I fool around with Tyler after I've had a few. I have to bring my toothbrush and mouthwash with me though so I don't get caught when I come home and, well, for other reasons. Tyler's applied to the college and he should know soon if he's been accepted. I am so glad he decided to stay in town so we can be together. He's also going to live on campus, which I think is pretty cool I hear they have some awesome parties in the dorms. They also have a campus pub, but they're really strict with IDs and you have to have their college ID and a license that prove you are 21 to get served. Most people just go to Shoprite liquors and get kegs to bring in the dorm. Anyway, I'm glad I live in walking distance from the radio station. TW and Chris gave me a curfew extension to 11:30 on Friday nights so that Tyler can walk me home. I'm trying to stay on their good sides. The house is looking pretty clean, I must say. Plus, I am keeping my grades up so I am being recommended for honors again next year. We still do the Poetry Club, but it's getting kind of boring and without Tyler next year I may quit. The only thing that worries me these days is Gram. She keeps complaining about being tired and having heartburn. TW and Chris and I are going to visit her next Sunday. I hope she's OK. Chris has been in a good mood lately which helps, too. I think it's because he got some good contracting jobs and is busy working a lot, and when he's not working he's at meetings and when he's home he's tired so he leaves me alone, thank God. And if Chris is in a good mood, TW is in a good mood. She told me we need to make sure he follows his program and does not relapse. I think she should worry about herself, but then again, she keeps getting all these AA sobriety chips so I guess she's fine. And she has like three sponsees that she talks to. Hey, a busy TW and Chris make my life easier for sure!

February 4th, 1985

Gram had a heart attack and died today! I can't believe it. TW and Chris signed me out of school and we're in Warwick. I am in shock. I know she had been having heartburn, but I didn't think it was a heart attack. The doctor at the hospital said that symptoms in women are often milder and different than in men and that heart attacks in women can often be fatal. I just can't believe she's gone. I mean, she wasn't even that old and she was so full of life. She was like a mother to me, and then TW took me away and now she is dead. I wish I had spent more time with her. I've been so busy with school and Tyler and Joni and I took her for granted. Now I feel so guilty. Maybe if I had spent more time with her she'd still be here. Maybe she wore herself out living alone. TW doesn't even seem that upset. She and Chris are taking care of the arrangements and she hasn't cried once. At least in front of me. I am a wreck. I don't know how I am going to face everyone for the viewing. I hope I can keep it together. It feels like I lose everyone important in my life and now all I have is Tyler and Joni. Now there really is no reason for me to go back to Warwick. We have the viewing tomorrow and Wednesday and the funeral is Thursday. Then Chris and TW will take me home and they asked Joni's mom if I could stay with her for two weeks while they clean out the townhouse and put it on the market and all that stuff. How can they be so cold? I walked in there and saw all of Gram's stuff, things I grew up with, and they are just going to sell it all, or donate it and it will be gone. They said I can have a piece of her jewelry to remember her by, and a photo album she had of me as a baby, that has her and Gramps. That's it. That's all I'll have left of her. I am so sad. I miss her so much.

February 22nd, 1985

Well, I made it through the viewing and funeral. Somehow. All of Gram's friends from the townhouse community were there, plus her church friends and even the mayor. A lot of people loved her. Oh, and Kyle and his parents came, and so did Julia with her baby girl, who cried the whole time and she had to leave. Kyle and his parents were nice, they hugged me and told me how sorry they were. I had to let Julia hug me, too. She gave the baby to her mother to hold. I couldn't wait for her to leave. Oh, and she and Kyle broke up. She's going to the pregnant school and is a single mother. Kyle has a new girlfriend. Whatever. I miss Gram. I'm just glad that I never have to go back to Warwick. There is nothing left for me there. Nothing. Joni and Tyler have been trying to comfort me, and Joni's mom was nice to me while I was there, but I feel like a part of me is missing. I've just been going through the motions at school. Tyler and Joni begged me to go to the radio station tonight to hang out on Tyler's show, and I'm going but I really don't feel like it. And I don't feel like doing what Tyler is going to want me to do. I wish he was OK with just holding me and making out, but once we start that he always wants more. But I'd rather be with him and Joni than TW and Chris. So I'm going. Tyler thinks I should get high. He thinks it will take my mind off things. There's a door that leads out of the bathroom to the roof where he smokes. I don't really see how getting high is going to help, but he swears by it. Maybe he's right. When he goes out there with Joni and Jason, they all come back giggly. They think everything is funny. Right now I don't think anything is funny. At all.

March 15th, 1985

So Joni sat me down after school yesterday and had a talk with me. She told me that she loves me and all and that she understands that I am upset about Gram, but that I am bringing everybody down and I'm going to lose Tyler if I don't snap out of it. I know she's right, but how do I just turn off how I feel? Joni says pot does it for her. And she says it makes sex really good. She and Jason are doing it. Now that he has his license, since he turned 17 in January, he drove her to the free clinic in Morristown and she got on the pill. She says that it takes about a month to work so you have to use condoms until your first period. She also said that she was afraid about gaining weight, because everyone says that happens, but she only gained a couple of pounds and her clothes still fit, and now she knows exactly when she gets her period every month. That is definitely a plus. I never know when I am going to get mine and I get cramps really bad when I do. I know I need to get over Gram dying but it is hard. Drinking relaxes me but doesn't make me feel happy. It's Joni's weekend to go to her dad's so I asked TW and Chris if I can take the bus into the city on Saturday. I'm going to hang out with Tyler at the radio station tonight. He still wants me to try out being a DJ for an hour but I'm kind of nervous. Maybe after I have a beer I'll let him put me on mic. I'm going to have to treat him special to make up for my bad mood over the past few weeks. Otherwise I'm afraid he's going to break up with me and start going out with some college girl. There's this one girl who's a freshman that keeps showing up to flirt with him. He says he's not into her, but if Joni's worried then I guess I should be. Anyway, Joni wants me to smoke with her this weekend. She knows where her dad keeps his stash. I was like, wait, your dad is a hippie? And she said, no, everyone his age smokes pot. Everyone? Not TW and Chris. They are the same age and they're all about being straight. She is so lucky she has a cool dad. She said he also went to Woodstock. I guess that was a pretty big deal back then. She's named Joni after Joni Mitchell. So what I don't get is that at school they are all about "Just say no" and how drugs are evil and will destroy your life. But how come Joni's dad has a good job and an apartment and seems like a perfectly nice guy and he smokes pot? Anyway,

Joni says it will help my bad mood so I'm going to give it a try. And I think I'm going to ask Tyler to take me to Morristown so I can get on the pill. The senior/junior prom is in May and he wants me to go and spend the night at the shore with him. I'm going to have to figure out how to do that. If Joni goes with Jason I have an excuse because I can say we're at her dad's. I wish I was older and had more freedom. It is such a pain in the ass to have to be lying all the time and sneaking around, just to be with my friends and boyfriend. My whole life would be so much easier if I was 18, not 14 about to turn 15. Tyler turns 18 in July. There are some states where it's legal to drink at 18. But not here.

March 20th, 1985

So I got high for the first time. Joni told me that I wouldn't feel it the first time that I smoked but I did. We were sitting in her bedroom in her dad's apartment and I was sitting on her dresser. We smoked a bowl (that's what she calls it) and it made me cough but I was able to hold the smoke. Anyway, at first I didn't feel anything so I thought she was right about the first time. But then 15 minutes later it kicked in. It felt like the dresser was levitating. I was like, oh, so that's why they call it being high. So I said to Joni, hey, I feel like I'm in *The Wizard of Oz.* She was like, what are you talking about? And I said, I feel like the dresser is up in the air. She didn't believe me, she thought I was joking. She was like there is no way you are high. I was like uh, well I feel like I'm in *The Wizard of Oz.* Then she wanted to listen to some music so we put on "Third Rail Emergency Power Trip" by Rain Parade. She's getting more into the trippy stuff Tyler likes. We both laid down on the floor and just let the music wash over us. Everything felt more there. Like the musical notes were more intense and powerful and the album sounded better than it ever had before. We were lying there stoned for a while and then Joni said, "Let's go down to the deli on the corner and get cookies,

I'm hungry." I was like all paranoid and said but won't they know we're stoned? She was like, they don't care. They just want to sell us cookies. I love NYC. You can just be who you want to be. So we went down and spent like 15 minutes trying to decide which cookies to buy. It was a tough decision and we were laughing and the guy behind the counter (who probably didn't speak English anyway) just ignored us. So we finally decided to buy Fudgetowns and went back up to her dad's apartment and put on *Saturday Night Live*. Her dad was still out, Joni said sometimes he stays over at his girlfriend's house if it gets late. *Saturday Night Live* was so funny. And the cookies tasted better than they ever have. We eventually got tired and went to sleep in her room. Her dad was home when we woke up, but thank God Joni put the stash back and aired out her room before we went to bed. He was in a good mood the next morning and took us out for brunch so I don't think he knows anything. So, now I get it. How pot does make you feel better. Why is it that everything that feels good adults say is bad? Like sex and pot. It's like they don't want us to have any fun. And people go to jail for smoking pot. I don't get it. It's not like it makes people violent or anything. It's not like heroin. I've seen junkies in Washington Square, all strung out and pathetic. How is pot the same as that? Joni says coke is good too, but it's really expensive. Her Dad's not into coke so we can't try that unless the guys have some and I don't think that's their thing. So, next weekend the four of us are going to see *The Breakfast Club* movie since it's finally coming to H'town. I heard it's really good.

March 24th, 1985

So we went to see *The Breakfast Club* last night. It was good. They got the different high school cliques down well, except there is no way a bunch of kids would get stoned in a high school in the library? Really? I mean it makes a good story, but I just can't see that happening. At all. Especially in our school. I mean, teachers are everywhere. You get suspended for smoking a cigarette on school grounds. Pot? They'd have the police there and you'd probably get sent to one of those rehab places or reform school. That happened to this guy Larry. He was one of the metal stoners and he got caught smoking pot in the woods behind the school and it was a big deal. Cops came and we all had to go to an assembly to hear about the evils of marijuana. Well, it was kind of stupid for him to smoke it at school. Besides who would want to sit in class stoned? That sounds like a dumb idea and not very much fun. Anyway, he's gone. Off to some rehab somewhere. So, speaking of school, I've been getting behind on my work and TW and Chris are on me so I'm going to have to be good this weekend and stay home and do chores and my work. They said if I get everything done I can go up to the station with Tyler next week. They didn't ground me from him, thank God, but I can only see him in school until all my work is done. He's being cool about it though. Especially because he's going to take me to Morristown for an appointment at the free clinic so I can get on the pill. TW and Chris don't know, of course. Can you imagine? But hey, would they rather me get pregnant? I mean everyone is scared about AIDS and I get that, but I don't think Tyler is cheating on me. He calls me every night from home and I don't think his parents would let him sneak girls into his room. And if he did, he wouldn't be calling me! Ugh I don't want to think about that. Especially since he got into the college and is going to be staying in the dorm in September. He is so lucky! I can't believe his parents are letting him do that when he lives so close to the school. But his dad is a lawyer and has money and they want him to have the college experience. Sophomore year is going to be so boring without him. I am definitely quitting Poetry Club next year. Especially since we have more freedom to move around at lunch.

April 22nd, 1985

So we just finished spring break and I got stuck at home for most of it because I had a book report due for English and a project due for History and two lab reports for Science, and of course the teachers all gave us homework that was due when we got back because we're honors and supposed to do more than everyone else. My grades have slipped to Bs because I'm having a hard time keeping up with everything. Tyler did take me to Morristown last month to get the pill and I have been making sure to take it every day. I don't think it's making me fat, but my boobs have gotten bigger and I had to get new bras. Tyler likes that side effect. So in a couple of days I should get my period and then I'm good to go. I'm kind of nervous because Joni said it hurts the first time. Tyler said he'd be gentle though. He wants me to like it. I hope it's better than what I do for him now. I really don't like doing that at all, but it keeps him from cheating on me, I think. I mean, he says he loves me, but Joni gets me all insecure because she says that guys drop girls who don't put out. I want to believe that Tyler is deeper than that. I mean, he and I have really interesting conversations about all kinds of stuff. Except when we get stoned. I've decided that I like pot better than alcohol. I hate being hungover and getting sick (which happens if I drink too much), and I never know how much is going to be too much until it's too late. Pot relaxes me (except sometimes it makes me paranoid) and it makes me laugh, and it does take my mind off of Gram. I still miss her, but it's gotten easier. Anyway, the other night I was finally allowed to go out because I finished all the work I owed. So I met Tyler at the radio station. He took me out to the roof to get high and then when we came back in to the studio he put me on mic! I wasn't prepared at all and didn't know what to say and kept forgetting what I wanted to say. He was like, just tell people what music they heard, but I made an ass out of myself because I couldn't remember all the songs and who did them. So he turned my mic off. I was kind of annoyed but since I was stoned I wasn't that annoyed and then the whole thing seemed kind of funny. So, he put on a couple of long songs so we could fool around and right in the middle Joni and Jason walked in! I was like Oh. My. God. But they just thought it was funny and went down to the lounge. It kind of ruined the mood so we stopped. Then we got high again with all of us together and when we got back Tyler put Jason on mic. He sounded like a jerk. I don't really like Jason, but he's Joni's boyfriend so I put up with him. He dropped out of Poetry Club because he thinks it's lame. And now Joni dropped out, so I am thinking I might as well drop out, too. I mean, the other kids are OK, but I can't really relate to them because they are too straight and honor-studenty. Is that a word? Anyway, I like it better when I hang out with Joni without Jason and of course I love to be alone with Tyler but it's never just me and Joni and Tyler. Jason is always there. I am so glad that Tyler's show is at night. None of the professors or the student managers are around so we have the place to ourselves. Well, I have to go do more homework or they'll start calling TW. And I want to make sure I can go to the prom with Tyler next month. I've already gotten permission and I told TW and Chris that I'm going to stay in the city with Joni for the whole weekend, so I have a cover. Tyler's got a room down in Seaside Heights for us and he promised that it was just for us, not a bunch of seniors to party in. I think most of the senior class is going to be staying in Seaside Heights that night. I guess it is a tradition. I don't care about them, I just want to be with Tyler.

May 5th, 1985

Oh. My. God. Tyler and I did it this weekend. TW and Chris were out at some AA thing and we were able to be alone in the house without them knowing after Tyler got out of work. It hurt a little at first, but we smoked before we did it so I would be relaxed. Tyler was gentle like he promised. And it actually ended up feeling pretty good. Much better than what I was doing for him before. Especially because I enjoy it too. He had to sneak out of the window when TW and Chris came home. Thank God he only lives a couple of blocks away. I pretended to be asleep when they got home (it was like 11 or something) and aired out the room, so all was cool. I can't wait to do it again! Tyler's parents don't get home from work until like 6 p.m. on weekdays so I'm going to tell TW and Chris that I'm going to his house to study. His mom just got a job at the mall but they don't know that so they think she's going to be home. Plus, both TW and Chris are out working at that time anyway, so as long as I'm home by 5:30 for dinner I'm good. If I make sure I do homework during lunch I think I can get away with it. Most of the classes that give homework I have in the morning so that should work. I will miss hanging out with Joni at lunch but she's with Jason most of the time anyway. Her dad is away with his girlfriend in France or something so she has not been going to NYC. We usually all hang out on Friday nights at the radio station and then Tyler and I do our own thing on Saturday nights after he gets off work. Now that it's getting warmer it's easier to find places to park. There is this rest area off Route 80 that we really like. And since I've been doing my work TW and Chris said they'll raise my curfew to midnight starting on my birthday. They are going to take me and Tyler out to this nice restaurant in town. Chris has been in a really good mood lately so that helps. And they finished everything they had to take care of with Gram's estate. Apparently Gram left TW a lot of money. And when there's money TW and Chris are happy. And a happy TW and Chris means more freedom for me!

May 19th, 1985

Well, I am now 15. My actual birthday fell on a Friday, which is good because Tyler and I got to spend it alone after school doing you know what. I love him so much. I never thought I would love anyone as much as Kyle, but I am so over him. Anyway, then we went to the radio station so he could do his show and he found this record in the library that had a 30-minute song, which was long enough to sneak out to the roof to smoke and go to the lounge, and well, you know. It was the best birthday I have had in a while. He gave me a birthday gift on Saturday night when we went out to dinner with TW and Chris. A gold bracelet with our names engraved on it! I don't want to take it off. I am so glad TW and Chris like him. It makes my life so much easier. If they only knew. They think he's such a goody two shoes, it is really funny. All because he is college bound and has a father who's a lawyer. So I ended up quitting Poetry Club because finals are coming up in a couple of weeks and I need all my lunch periods to study. I'm still pulling B's, but I told TW and Chris that I quit in order to make sure I keep my grades up. They believed that, so good. School will be out soon anyway and now the prom is coming up. TW said she'll take me to the mall to get a dress this weekend because the prom is Friday, May 28th. So I already told her that Tyler, Joni, Jason and I are taking a limo to the prom, which is in Secaucus near the city. What I didn't tell her is that I am not staying over at Joni's house for the weekend. As long as she doesn't call there, which she doesn't usually do (I don't think she has Joni's dad's number, but I guess she could get it from Joni's mom), I should be good to go. The water at Seaside Heights is going to be too cold to swim so I'm not packing a suit or anything. But I don't think we were going swimming anyway, hah! Memorial Day weekend is coming up and TW and Chris want to go away by themselves. I actually convinced them that I could stay alone in the house. I have no idea how I did that! But it is awesome!! Now I can spend the whole weekend with Tyler!! Other kids I know like to throw parties when their parents go away, but I just don't really like parties. I would rather just be with Tyler or a couple of close friends. Besides, those kids get really stupid and annoying when they're drunk. Isn't it funny how other people are annoying when they're drunk and you aren't, but when you are they just seem normal? Anyway, I would rather just be with Tyler, have sex, listen to music and get stoned. I've been building up my album collection slowly with the money I get for allowance and doing chores. I'll have more money coming in this summer because I got a job at the concession stand at the pool. The pool opens at 10 a.m. and I have to be there from 10-3 p.m., and then the second shift takes over. So I'll be able to go be with Tyler after. He is going to be doing some lawn mowing in addition to his job at the record store, but his hours are 7-2 p.m. so that works out perfectly.

Tuesday, May 28th, 1985

What an awesome weekend I just had!! I spent the whole weekend with Tyler (except for during the day Saturday when he was working, then I hung out with Joni). We got away with it. TW and Chris never suspected a thing. I was always home when they called and Tyler helped me clean up the house on Monday, so it was spotless when they came back and TW was thrilled. I can't wait for the prom and I get to spend the weekend with Tyler again!! Then one more week of regular school and then finals week. I don't have to start work until June 22nd because that's when the pool opens. Joni got her dress for the prom. It's pink and matches her hair. Speaking of which, mine started to grow out and I'm not that into punk anymore anyway, so TW let me go to the hairdresser in town and get it colored close to my natural color. It's layered so it can grow out from the punk cut. So I can get any color dress now. Not that I couldn't before, but anyway. I have to remember to pack my pills. I've been keeping them hidden in the closet in my room because TW never goes in there. I'm probably going to have to party with the seniors after the prom for a bit, but Tyler promised me we'd be alone after that. The seniors are OK, I guess. Except when they're hammered. Some of them are just pigs. They try to get girls drunk and have sex with them. I mean, just random girls, not like girlfriends. I think that's gross. I mean, it's one thing if you're in a relationship but to just use someone for sex? At least they know not to hit on me, because they know I'm with Tyler. I really can't imagine having sex with someone I didn't have feelings for. I just don't get how that is fun. Especially if the guy is sloppy drunk. But some girls don't care. They just get wasted and do whatever. Anyway, I do plan on having some champagne in the limo before the prom, but that's about it.

June 10th, 1985

It's finals week and I've been so busy since the prom that I haven't had time to write. I pulled off going to the shore for the weekend! I am getting good at this! So the prom was OK. I ended up getting a green dress to match my eyes and TW took pictures of us before the limo came. We had champagne in the limo but it didn't really hit me too much, so I was good when we got there. I don't really get what people like so much about proms. The food was so-so and the music was lame. I was glad to get out of there by the end. But at least we looked nice. Anyway, by the time we got to Seaside Heights it was about 2 a.m. and then Tyler wanted to party with his friends and so did Joni and Jason, so we didn't go back to our room until 5 a.m. and then slept until like 3 p.m. the next day. We got up and went out for something to eat and then spent the rest of the day in the room catching up on well, you know. Then we got a ride from one of Tyler's friends back home on Sunday. My favorite part of the weekend was being with Tyler. The partying part was just what I thought it would be. Those seniors like to drink. The ones who went to the prom don't smoke pot, so Tyler and I snuck away with Joni and Jason. Pot kind of makes me go into myself, so I just sat in a corner and watched people. I didn't really talk to anyone because I don't really know most of the seniors and the people who were there were the jocks and cheerleader crowd. I don't know why Tyler wanted to go, except that I guess he didn't want to miss out on his senior prom. The whole thing seemed like a waste of money to me. I would rather have just gone to the shore with Tyler for the weekend. Oh well. The things we do for love. And I do love him. I'm going to graduation to see him graduate and then his parents are taking us to dinner at some fancy place in Allamuchy. I had to get another dress for that, too. But it's OK. I'm just happy to be with him.

June 26th, 1985

Chris got injured on the worksite and has to stay home for a couple of months. This is not good. He's in a really bad mood, and in pain because he won't take pain killers because of AA. He's picking on me all the time and complaining about everything. TW just takes it. She waits on him hand and foot like she's his slave, when she's home that is. I try to stay out of his way and do what he says. Nothing good happens when Chris is in a bad mood. They want me to go with them to some Fourth of July family reunion his family is having at somebody's farm up in Sussex or Wantage or someplace like that. Thank God I have to work at the pool because they need extra people for the holiday. I'll be working during the day but will have the evening off. But, since Chris is out of work for a while and we're living just on TW's money from her job (she doesn't want to use her inheritance and she and Chris had a big fight about that one, because of bills) he is not making me take off from work. Speaking of big fights, he and TW have really been going at it lately. She wants him to go to more meetings and is calling him a dry drunk. What is a dry drunk? It sounds like a contradiction. He yells at her and tells her not to tell him what to do and to take her own inventory, whatever that means. TW is now going to Al-Anon meetings in addition to AA to deal with Chris. So, she's out. A lot. And guess who has to deal with Chris? I thought I was going to spend every day with Tyler, but Chris wants me home to do housework. Like I'm the maid. Oh, and then cook dinner when TW is out. I told TW I don't want to do that and she said I don't have to on the weekends just during the week when she is at meetings. I'm doing it so that at least I can be with Tyler on the weekends. TW's been making Chris go to meetings with her on Saturdays and Sundays. So now, even though school is out, I am seeing Tyler less. He still calls me every night, though.

July 5th, 1985

TW and Chris came home early yesterday. They left the reunion early because they got in a fight. So not only was Chris in a horrible mood when they got home, but Tyler was still here (I had gotten off work at 6 p.m.). Thank God we weren't doing anything or smoking. Now that it's warm out we just go outside to smoke. But boy was Chris pissed. He was screaming at me and Tyler and told me to stop acting like a whore. A whore? We weren't even doing anything except watching TV. In fact, we were going to go out and see the fireworks. If they had just come home a little later then we would have been fine. He made Tyler leave and proceeded to yell at me and tell me what an ungrateful bitch I was. I swear to God. He went on and on about how I take everything he and TW do for granted and should be grateful that I live in his house. His? I thought it was theirs? He said since I didn't obey the rules, I was grounded for two weeks, except from work. Two weeks? Alone in the house with him? He said I will have extra chores and that if they are not done on time and properly I would be grounded for another week. I really hate him. And I hate TW for just standing there and not saying a word. He hasn't hit me yet, but I see it coming. He loves to go on and on about how when he was my age, if he didn't make his bed properly or do his chores on time his parents made him sleep in the doghouse. I've met them a couple of times and they seemed normal. But sleep in a doghouse? What kind of people did he come from? I know he said his father was a drunk but stopped drinking on his own and thinks anyone who can't do that is weak. His father used to beat him with a belt for things like not finishing his dinner or not taking out the garbage. Why did TW have to marry this guy? Of all the men she could have picked, she picked this asshole. And not even my dad. I still want to know who he is. I wish there was a way I could find out. Maybe I could go live with him. But then I'd have to leave Tyler. Now Tyler and I will have to sneak around for the next two weeks. No going to the radio station, either. Work and home. Everyday. And Chris said if I'm not home 15 minutes after I finish work, he will add a week of grounding for each time I am late. I feel like I'm under house arrest. Criminals have more freedom than me. Well, maybe not, but this is going to be torture. In fact, it already is.

July 21st, 1985

Freedom at last! TW and Chris actually let me go to the shore this weekend with Tyler and his parents. I had the weekend off from work since I put in extra hours in the past two weeks. It was better than staying home with Chris and now I have some extra money. We just got back a little while ago. It was so nice to just hang out on the beach with Tyler. We swam for a bit and then walked around the boardwalk and ate fried dough. I think this coming weekend we're going to go to the movies with Joni and Jason on Saturday, and then we'll go hang out by the swimming hole at the river. Somebody usually makes a bonfire at night and has pot. And there are places Tyler and I can sneak off to go be together. We don't want to take any chances with him getting caught in the house. Besides, I can go to his house after work now so we get to be alone then. Chris seems a bit calmer. I think he might be drinking again but I can't prove it. TW has no idea. She lives in her la-la land thinking life is wonderful. I don't know where he is hiding his alcohol. I don't see any beer bottles. Neither of them minds if I stay out to 12:30 a.m.

as long as I'm up for work, so maybe I can enjoy the rest of the summer. Once school starts Tyler will be in the dorm and he doesn't have late afternoon classes. I hope his roommate doesn't either. I am going to have to be really good about being home by dinner and getting my homework done. But it's summer now and school feels really far away. I just want to enjoy my summer.

July 27th, 1985

Tyler's birthday was yesterday. We spent it at the radio station with Joni and Jason and got really high. I gave Tyler a you-know-what for his birthday since it has been a while. He really liked that. We are going out to dinner tonight with his parents for his official 18th birthday celebration, somewhere in Morristown at some fancy restaurant where I have to wear a dress. I went shopping earlier and found one at the mall. TW took me so we could bond. She is worried that she hasn't spent enough time alone with me. She also told me that she is worried about Chris. She thinks he's drinking but she can't prove it. I mean, wouldn't she smell it on his breath? But he chews this violet gum so it's hard to tell. I kind of like him better these days because he is less uptight. He sleeps more during the day, too. He's not back to work yet and TW is starting to get annoyed. Supposedly, the doctor says he can go back to work at the end of August, but he doesn't seem too eager. Why should he be when he has a rich wife who works and does whatever he wants? I am never going to marry a man like that. TW is such a slave. And she tells me how much she loves him and how he is the best thing that ever happened to her and blah, blah, blah. Well, just wait until she catches him drinking. WWIII for sure. And I know he is. I found a bottle of Wild Turkey in the trash. He doesn't know I know. Anyway, I have to get ready for dinner with Tyler and his parents. I'm going to give him a real gift tonight. I got him a gift certificate to the store in the mall that sells stereo components. This way he can upgrade his stereo for college. I used a lot of my pool money, but he's worth it. When I am with him I don't think about TW and Chris or Gram. I still miss her though.

August 10th, 1985

Tyler's been away with his parents at the shore all week. He gets home tomorrow. Joni is with her Dad for the month in the Hamptons and she invited me, but I have no way to get there. Life has been incredibly boring this past week. All I have to do is work. Except it's been rainy with thunderstorms and when that happens they close the pool so I had less hours. Which means I've been home with Chris. Even though Chris is almost ready to go back to work he seems even lazier. All he does is sit in front of the TV. He doesn't even hide his drinking from me anymore, since I caught him. He made me promise not to tell TW and said that if I did he would ground me for the rest of the summer. It doesn't even matter if I'm doing chores or not, he said he will find a reason. I hate him! TW is completely blind. She just goes to work, meetings and spends her free time on the phone. They barely spend time together except at dinner. I don't know why she puts up with it. I don't see him looking for work either. He's cleared to go back to work soon and he doesn't have any jobs lined up. So now he and TW fight about that. You know, I think she knows he's drinking again anyway, but just not admitting it. Al-Anon tells her not to confront him and not to enable him. I don't see how that helps. He just continues to drink either way and sit on his ass all day. This has been a long week. At least Tyler's coming home. Joni won't be home until school starts. I have summer reading I have to do for English so I went to the library to do that. I was so bored this week that I finished my book report as well. At least I don't have to worry about that. I've heard that the honors classes are even more work this year because they're getting us ready for AP classes junior and senior year. I'm thinking of getting out of honors because I have to spend too much time on work already, and if I want to keep Tyler I have to make sure I have time to see him. The only class I like is English anyway. Plus, in honors a C is failing. If I go into regular classes and I get a C it's fine. I know kids who get C's and still go to college. It may be county, but it's still college. I'm sick of doing what adults want me to do. Especially when I watch Chris lying around the house all day doing nothing. When I'm with Tyler I forget about my boring life and all is right with the world. I don't think about Chris and his drinking, or miss Gram. It's going to be really hard to get used to a regular school schedule again. I think I'm going to see my guidance counselor and switch my classes to regular except for English. Then I really can get my homework done at lunch and be free after school. TW is going to be pissed off because I'm dropping most of the honors classes. She was already pissed about me dropping out of Poetry Club. But she'll forget about it. She has enough other things to worry about. Especially if Chris does not go back to work. At least I'll be out of the house all day every day.

September 3rd, 1985

School started today. It's really lonely here without Tyler and now without Joni. She decided to live with her dad in the city and go to private school there because she's sick of living in the sticks. She and Jason broke up, too. I haven't seen much of her lately anyway. I guess I could go visit her in the city, but then I wouldn't get to spend weekends with Tyler. I did switch to regular classes, even for English, because in order to get my required classes the only time honors English was offered was at the same time as Bio and that is required. Well, now that I have nobody to hang out with at lunch at least I can get my homework done then. TW was pissed about me dropping out of honors, but she's been distracted because the first day Chris finally went back to work, he went to a bar afterwards and got drunk and then got in an accident and lost his license for a year, so now he's back home again. So not only does TW have to support him but she has to drive him everywhere, too. I don't want to be in that house any more than I have to. Tyler started school. He's still doing his radio show on Friday nights so I can still go up there to hang out. Plus, his roommate goes home every weekend!! So we can have the room to ourselves. I just have to figure out what to tell Chris and TW. They'll get suspicious if I tell them I'm going to Joni's in the city every weekend. They know she and I are not that close. But at least I can spend most of my weekends with Tyler. He kept his job at the record store on Saturdays. Maybe they need more help and I can work there, too. Anyway, I am trying to hatch up a plan. Tyler's dorm is co-ed so I can say I made friends with one of the girls there and say I'm staying with her overnight and then stay with Tyler instead. I'll just tell TW and Chris that I'm doing that. Oh, and TW wanted to clean out my closet the other day. I had to act fast and tell her I'd do it myself because I don't want her to find my pills. Plus, I have some pot that Tyler gave me. So I spent all day yesterday cleaning out and re-organizing my closet. TW was thrilled.

September 16th, 1985

I just got back from spending the weekend with Tyler and all hell has broken loose at home. But maybe that's a good thing because nobody said a word when I told them I was staying at my new friend Sharon's dorm at the college. I just told TW and Chris that I had this new friend (only partially a lie) who I met at Tyler's dorm and she said I could stay over. We spent Friday night at the radio station and then went to a dorm party Saturday night that was on Sharon's floor actually, and I came home Sunday, no questions asked. Chris was already passed out on the couch when I got home about 5 p.m. I helped TW make dinner and then told her I was going upstairs to do homework. Which I did and then smoked a joint and aired out the room. Since TW and Chris have been fighting so much I find it helps me relax. I've been afraid he's going to hit her. Now that he's drinking again his temper is really bad after he gets drunk. He's been getting rides to and from his work site with friends and he was home early today. TW came home early, too, for some reason and found him on the couch watching TV. She asked him why he was home early and bam, another fight started. Chris got fired for drinking on the job and TW was mad! She mouthed off to him and he hauled off and smacked her. I swear to God. I've been afraid this would happen. TW ran off to their bedroom and told Chris he was sleeping on the couch until further notice. She locked the door and started calling her Al-Anon friends. Chris was just muttering to himself about what a bitch TW is. I made myself dinner and went up to my room, rolled a joint and called Tyler. My nerves are shot from those two. I wish I could just move in with Tyler. My life would be so much easier. Even though my classes are easier than last year I just can't concentrate.

September 23rd, 1985

I cut school last Tuesday to be with Tyler and he skipped class as well. It was awesome! Well, until the school called my house to see why I was absent and Chris answered the phone. When I came home he just started screaming at me. He was like asking me what the hell was the matter with me and why I was so disrespectful and told me I was an ungrateful bitch. I lost it and told him to go fuck himself and that he was a useless drunk who was being supported by my mother. He hauled off and smacked me across the face, really hard. Then I really had to stay home from school for the rest of the week because I was all black and blue, and TW was afraid that somebody at school would call DYFS. I've been under house arrest since then and now that Chris is home all day he watches me like a hawk. They took away my stereo and won't let me out of the house or use the phone. I can't even call Tyler and he has called here worried about me and they won't let him speak to me. They grounded me from him for the rest of the month. I have to sit at the kitchen table and do my work and TW checks it when she gets home. Chris told me that if I disobey either of them, cut school again or give them any trouble he will beat me black and blue with a belt and he doesn't care about DYFS. I told him he is abusive and he was like, "Oh yeah? Call DYFS yourself." I hate him and I hate TW more for doing whatever he says. At least they haven't taken my journal yet, but I've decided to hide it in a better place. I found an old jewelry box in my closet that has a key and I keep the key on me at all times. I also moved my pot and pills to it. Smoking is keeping me sane. I am so stressed out. I actually am looking forward to going to school Monday so I can get out of this house. TW is making me go to her Al-Anon meetings with her this weekend and she's staying home to keep an eye on me. And, Chris is still drinking and she says nothing. Nothing. I get blamed for all the shit going on in this house. If there are dishes in the sink, if my room is not clean, and if the laundry isn't done. Oh yeah, they gave me extra chores as well. Now I have to clean the bathrooms and kitchen and do the laundry. I am their fucking slave. I hate them. I was able to sneak a call to Tyler at like 3 a.m. when they were asleep just to let him know what's going on. He feels bad for me, but what can he do? They also want to meet my new friend from the college. TW says she's worried about me hanging out with older kids, especially at the dorm where there is drinking. Um, but she's not worried about me being home with drunken Chris all day? What planet is she on? I swear sometimes she is so stupid and naive. Which works in my favor sometimes, but not now. I am dreading going to all those meetings this weekend. The people in them are always so overdramatic and they all sound the same. They complain and then they say but thank God for the program, they don't know what they would do without it. TW stopped going to

AA meetings. Now she is all about Al-Anon. She says the 12-Steps are the 12-Steps and she needs her support. It's not like I could call Tyler anyway because she's always on that fucking phone when she gets home from work. Half the time we eat pizza unless I cook.

October 14th, 1985

So I finally got out of house jail last Friday and TW and Chris let me go to the station to be with Tyler, but they won't let me stay over at the dorm until they meet this girlfriend. I'm too embarrassed to ask her to come over to meet them, and they'll just ask a bunch of questions and I'll get busted for sure. I miss Joni. She hasn't returned my calls and has a new life and new friends in NYC, so all I have is Tyler. The kids at school are lame. Now that I'm in regular classes there's nobody good to hang out with or talk to. All they care about is football games and their hair (the girls) and what parties they are going to. I can't relate to any of them. Oh, and then I thought things were better with TW and Chris because he started sleeping in their bedroom again and they weren't yelling at each other. He told her he had a job lined up and just needed to find a ride to and from work. TW has been trying to keep it together but I can tell she's about to lose it. She told Chris she is not going to dip into her savings and that he needs to get his act together. That's what her Al-Anon friends are telling her to do anyway. He talks a good game but then he goes back to drinking. He gets a job, holds on to it for a couple of days and then always gets fired. If this is what he was like with his first wife no wonder she doesn't have anything to do with him.

October 22nd, 1985

I am failing Math. They called home and got Chris and of course he was drunk and went off on me. No belt, thank

God, but still. Now I have to be home right after school every day and am only allowed to see Tyler on weekends until I get my Math grade up. And then when Chris told TW they got in a big fight because he told her I am out of control and that she doesn't do anything about it. She was like, well I work all day and I can't babysit my daughter. He told her she was a shitty parent and then she lost it and punched him in the face. Punched him in the face! I've never seen her like that. And it was a stupid thing to do because he really went after her then and threw her against the wall and beat the shit out of her. I was about to call the police it was that bad, and I was afraid he was going to turn on me. He left the house and I made sure that TW did not have any broken bones. I was going to call 911 but she said no, she was just badly bruised. Now she has to take some time off from work. I have no idea what she told them but she must have come up with something because she's been home since yesterday and is waiting for the bruises to heal some more so that she can cover them with make-up. Chris must have found somewhere to stay because he has not been home since they had the fight. I heard her talking to her Al-Anon sponsor and she was crying and saying she didn't know if she could take living with Chris anymore. Good. I hope she kicks him out. Things will be a lot better around here.

October 24th, 1985

Well, sure enough, Chris came home with a dozen roses and apologized up and down to TW and swore he would never hit her again. He pleaded with her to forgive him and he promised to get a real job and made us dinner, which he never does. And I am glad he never does because he can't cook for shit. I'm really worried because I'm still failing Math and I just can't concentrate. My other grades are starting to slip as well. Every time I try to study my mind wanders and I'm starting to have trouble following what we're doing in class, so I've been getting zeros on homework. I decided to just give up. The only time I feel good is when I'm with Tyler or when I'm stoned, and when TW and Chris find out I am still failing they'll take him away again. I'm starting to get all nervous now; I think I need to smoke.

November 4th, 1985

Report cards came out today and my life is over. I failed Math and have C's in everything else. It's not like I can concentrate at home anymore anyway. TW and Chris are constantly fighting and he still does not have a job. In fact, the only time they don't fight is when TW is at one of her meetings or on the phone with her Al-Anon friends. I was able to spend most of last weekend with Tyler; I even hung out with him at work. But now with this report card, which has to be signed, that's all over. Unless I can find a way to sneak out. Chris usually passes out in front of the TV and TW locks herself in the bedroom at night, so if I sneak out in the middle of the night and get home by morning they'll never know. I will try that this weekend because they're probably going to ground me for the rest of the year.

November 5th, 1985

I was right. My stereo is gone again, and I am under house arrest except for school. But I called Tyler from a pay phone at school and we have a plan. I'm going to sneak out on Friday and Saturday night to be with him. I have to get out of here.

November 10th, 1985

I didn't think my life could get worse, but it has. I got caught coming in this morning. I am grounded from everything except doing school work. All I'm allowed to do is read books, clean the house and do school work. I am so depressed. I don't know when I'll see Tyler again unless I cut school to do it, and I have to figure out how to do that without being caught. And since I can't leave the house I couldn't get my pills for this month. So on top of everything else I am feeling really moody from the hormones, and then three days after I ran out of pills I got my period really bad with cramps. And I can't get high because TW found my stash and flushed it down the toilet. TW sat me down for a talk. She told me that she's worried about my out-of-control behavior and that she thinks that I need to go away to a special boarding school. She said she talked to one of her Al-Anon friends who recommended this school that is a rehab for troubled kids. She scheduled an interview for me next week. And this place isn't even in New Jersey. It's somewhere in New York near the Pennsylvania border. I can't believe she wants to send me away. First she takes me out of my home with Gram and now she can't handle being married and a parent and I have to suffer for it? Chris told her that it's him or me. He told her he can't take living with me and that I am the reason he is drinking again. He really said that. And she is choosing him. She says it's for my own good but I see through her. She wants to save her marriage and she doesn't give a shit about me or what makes me happy. And I won't even be able to say goodbye to Tyler without sneaking around. I could try to run away, but where would I go? I can't stay at the college with Tyler, and Joni is gone. Maybe I am better off being at a boarding school. It can't be worse than living in this hellhole.

Some day in November

I am now officially in hell. I thought I was going to a nice private school in the country with some 12-Step meetings for the kids. This place is a worse jail than my house was. I am not even supposed to be writing in this journal; if staff find out then I am really in for it. I'm keeping it hidden in my moral inventory notebook. And what I had to do to get my journal back still makes me sick. But more about that later. TW drove me to the school for my interview on November 17th. It felt like it took forever to get there. We drove west into Pennsylvania in the middle of nowhere and ended up crossing state lines to some town called Deposit, NY. No deposit no return. And there is no return. I am here. For how long I don't know. Anyway, from the outside the school grounds looked like a sleepaway camp. Which at one time it was and then it got sold and made into this hellhole. TW drove up to the main building, which looked like a house. We got buzzed in by the front desk person who was a woman who looked like the grouchiest person I have ever seen. Then she picked up the phone and called someone and this girl who looked about Tyler's age shows up with her perfectly styled blonde hair and plaid skirt and button-down shirt with a preppy sweater tied around her shoulders. She smiled at us and said, "Oh, you must be Devon and Mrs. Anderson." TW corrected her and said, "Oh, it's Mrs. Downing now." I just rolled my eyes. Blondie led us down the hall to a room with a man who I swear had a toupee and was wearing a necktie. A polka-dotted neck tie. Who does that? So he dismisses Blondie and then has us take seats and shuts the door. "Welcome to Rolling Hills Academy," he says. "So, Mrs. Downing, what are your concerns about Devon and how can we help?" he asks. He doesn't even look at me. I could have been the wallpaper. TW launches into this whole story about how out of control I am and how I used to be this perfect honor student and now I smoke pot and I'm sneaking out of the house to have sex with an 18-year-old college boy and cutting school and it is tearing our family apart. And then she breaks down crying. And necktie pats her shoulder and says, "There, there, you have come to the right place. We will fix Devon up so that she's the girl you used to know, and you will be thrilled." TW is thanking him profusely, and telling him that she is at her wits' end and her marriage is failing and she didn't know what else to do. Meanwhile I'm just sitting there. Necktie looks at me and says, "Your mom and I are going to have a private chat." He picks up the phone and asks the front desk grouch to get Blondie back, except he called Blondie Kendall. Who names their kid after a male Barbie doll? That was the last I saw of TW. Literally. I was led into a small room with no furniture but a metal cabinet. There were two other girls in the room besides Kendall. I don't remember their names. I just know they were mean. Kendall looks at me and says, "You are no longer in control. We are. Take off your clothes." I looked at her and the other two girls. Were they serious? What kind of sick place is this? "Wait," I said, "I was just here for an interview, what is going on?" Kendall tells me, "No, you are staying here. We're going to cure you of your druggie ways." Wait, what?? I am thinking. Then she says, "I told you to take off your clothes. We have to do a strip search to make sure you aren't hiding drugs and we have to check your clothes." I didn't move. I wasn't going to strip in a room with these girls. Kendall, the preppie Barbie doll from hell, says to me, "Either you take your clothes off or we will." I still didn't move. All of a sudden the two other girls grab me by the arms and Kendall starts undressing me. What the fuck?? Who are these sickos? That was all I could think. So there I am standing in the nude in front of these girls. They start going through all of my clothes and even checking the seams to make sure I was not carrying any drugs. And then it got worse. They checked me. Cavity search. I just closed my eyes and pretended I was somewhere else. When they finished they didn't even give me my clothes back except for my bra and underwear. Kendall looked at me and said, "These clothes you came in with are part of your old life. Here are your new humble clothes." Humble clothes?? They handed me a sweat shirt, sweat pants, canvas shoes. Then Kendall said, "Keep them clean because laundry only gets done once a week." One of the Barbie clones left with my clothes and my journal which was in my pocketbook. Kendall grabbed my hand and said, "It's time for orientation." She put a leash around my wrist and grabbed the other end. She looked at me and said, "You can no longer go anywhere on your own. You are required to be monitored at all times and escorted at all times by a level three, including to the bathroom. You are a level one. That means you do what any level three, or staff, says. Got it?" "But..." I started to say, and she looked at me and said, "No talking without permission! Except to answer a question." Then she led me by the leash to the group room, which was in a separate building. I had to walk through the snow to get there and my canvas shoes, which were too big, got all wet and my feet were freezing. We got to the building, which still had a sign that said Rec Hall. She sat me down in a group of kids, boys and girls, and said, "Here is our newest level one. This is Devon." The kids all looked up in unison and said, "Hi, Devon," like a bunch of robots. Then Kendall says, "Who wants to tell Devon how things work?" Kendall, the Barbie, was in charge of the group. The doors to the Rec Hall were guarded by two male staff who were graduates of the program. There were no adults in the room. What kind of school was this? Some guy named Mike raises his hand and Kendall says, "Go ahead." He stands up and says, "You are here because you are a druggie. You have hurt your parents and messed up your life and theirs. But we will save you. You are so lucky to have been sent here. You will learn how to be a good person. We will make sure you no longer are influenced by druggie music, druggie clothes and druggie behavior. The first thing you need to do is accept that you are powerless and unable to manage your life. When you get honest and humble about your bad behaviors you will start to earn privileges. But not until then."

Then, because it was afternoon, it was time for Drug Education group. Barbie started the group by talking about how using pot and alcohol leads to destruction of the family, jail and death. I had never heard that pot killed anyone, but whatever. She said we were lucky because the program doesn't take kids who use hard drugs and that we should be grateful that we were caught early in our disease. Disease? I have a disease? She said that even using once or twice leads to addiction and that the disease is progressive. Then she asked for volunteers to talk about how their life was destroyed by drug use and why it made them into bad people. I felt like I had stepped into an alternate reality. All of the kids raise their hands, except me, waving them wildly trying to get picked to share. There were about 20 of us, all level one and two. You could tell who was on level one because they were wearing sweats and had a leash on their wrist. I counted about five of us. There were no level threes besides Barbie/Kendall. They have more freedom and get to go to school or work or help the office staff, or drag us level ones around all day as part of their service to the program. The boys all had crew cuts. The girls all had shoulder-length hair, combed straight and put back in a barrette. No bangs or any hair style that could block anyone's face so that eye contact could be made with the person speaking. But not with the opposite sex, unless that person was the speaker. I found that out because I turned around to look at the guys at the door and was told no eye contact with the opposite sex, no moving from my chair, and I must face forward to the speaker or leader at all times. You would think that was bad enough. But it just got worse from there. Whoever was picked (and you were expected to volunteer or be shamed) had to tell all the gory details about how they were bad people and how drugs made them bad. If the leader or anyone on level two thought the person was lying or in denial they got yelled at and told to get honest. Stories had to have detail. Barbie told us that because we are drug addicts we are liars and that is a symptom of the disease, so the only way to recover is to get ruthlessly honest. One kid talked about how he used drugs and had sex with a cow. And how drug use turned him into an evil person, and how he was a normal, church-going kid before he was using. He said when he used alcohol he became a sex addict. Everyone stood up and told him they loved him. And I thought cow tipping was bad. This went on and on for several hours, with each person volunteering some crazy behavior that was due to drugs. Each story got more and more crazy. And the crazier the story got the more excited the group got. Finally, (and thank God I was not called on) everyone was told to stand and sing some song about how great the program was and how it saves lives. Then all level ones were told to line up and wait for a level three to take hold of their leashes and lead them to the dining hall for dinner. I swear to God. Like we were a bunch of dogs. Oh, and no bathroom during group because that is avoiding. Once the level threes came to get us, we were led to the bathhouse where the level one bathrooms were and taken by a level three to the bathroom stall. There were no doors. We had to do our business while being watched by the level three person because we might try to run. I had to pee in front of one of the Barbies. With her looking at me. They gave us three minutes to do what we had to do, including wash up, and then they led us to dinner. Dinner was in the dining hall. Level ones were not allowed to talk and were given a plate with mystery meat, mashed potato and overboiled string beans. And a glass of water. That was it. Level twos got bread and choice of coffee or tea with their meal (decaf only). Level threes got to eat first and had a choice of meat, starch and veggie, choice of beverage and dessert. We were given a half hour to eat dinner and clean up the dining hall. Level threes got leave, except for the threes escorting level ones back to the bathroom before the next group. After the bathroom break we went back to the Rec Hall for evening group. This was to talk about the rules of the program. Since I was new I was handed a moral inventory journal. I was told that every night before bed I had to take my inventory and write about an experience I had using drugs that caused bad behavior, or I could write about how I ruined the lives of my family. The graduate guys were back at the door making sure no one would escape. Then it was time to go to our sleeping bunks. I was led by the leash to the level one girl's bunkhouse. There were eight of us. Inside were four bunk beds and a wooden cubby next to them for our things, which were our weekly issued clothes, underwear and journal and pen. There were no bathrooms and just bare mattresses with a blanket. We were given T-shirts to sleep in. The bunkhouse was not winterized so the only heat was a space heater in the corner. It gets pretty cold in upstate New York, but you don't get to sleep in a regular heated room until you are level two. A level three came in and told us we had an hour to write in our moral inventory journals. Then she left and locked the door from the outside so that we were locked in. There was no clock so I had no way of knowing when the hour was up, until the level three came back in. She said, "Time's up, lights out." Then she locked us in again. All the windows had locks and alarms as well, so there was no way to escape. Even to go to the bathroom. I put my MI journal in my cubby and tried to sleep. It was freezing in the bunkhouse and I couldn't stop my mind from going around and around. I finally got out of my bed which is on the bottom bunk and tapped the girl on the top bunk on the shoulder. "Hey," I asked, "what the hell is this place, anyway? I thought I was going to visit a new school and my mother just let them kidnap me?" She looked at me and said, "Shut the fuck up and go back to bed. You'll get in trouble for talking and get me in trouble. Just do what they tell you." I was like, holy shit this is not just jail it is a nut house. Somehow I fell asleep, and then it felt like as soon as I did, reveille was blasting from speakers outside and I had to pee. A level three opened the door to the bunkhouse, it was still dark outside. "Straighten up your things and line up for flagpole and breakfast," was all she said. We all had to make our beds, make sure our sleep tees were folded, and line up with our leashes on our wrists. By this time I really had to pee. Finally, level threes came to get us to take us to the bathhouse. I thought I was going to explode and at this point I didn't even care that someone was watching me pee. Then we had to line up at the sinks to wash up and a level three handed out toothbrushes and toothpaste and hairbrushes and barrettes. We were given three minutes to brush our teeth and put our hair back. Then we were led out to the flagpole where everyone had to meet before breakfast and say the pledge of allegiance after a level three raised the flag. We were led then to the dining hall for breakfast. Level ones got a glass of water and plain oatmeal. Level twos got orange juice, a choice of oatmeal or eggs, milk and decaf coffee or tea. Level threes got a choice of beverage, eggs, oatmeal with raisins and honey, or pancakes with syrup. They got served first. I took a bite of my oatmeal and almost gagged. It was disgusting! I decided not to eat it even though my stomach was growling. The other level ones were eating it and because of the no talking rule I couldn't ask them about it but I guess if you are hungry enough you eat anything. Finally breakfast was over and then it was back to the bathroom and time for morning group. Only level ones get morning group. Level threes have school or work (which can include leading us around) and level twos have independent study with a tutor in the main building. So, it was back to group to share our MI entries from the previous night. Sharing was required and we were locked in with the guys at the door again. Same deal as the other groups, face forward, no bathroom breaks, focusing on the speaker at all times. The first person who was picked shared about how she used drugs because her stepfather beat her and it helped her feel better. I guess that was the wrong thing to say because the level three leader (it was a guy this time, I don't know where Kendall/Barbie was) got right in her face and told her that she was not taking responsibility. He told her that she needed to admit why her step father was beating her, and that she deserved it and that using helped her avoid facing the consequences of her behavior and learning from them, so her stepfather had no choice but to beat her. She tried to explain that he did it because he was drinking, but that just made things worse. The level three called her some really nasty things and she ended up crying. Then he laughed and called her a baby. I thought about my inventory and realized that it was not bad enough and that the same thing would happen to me. I lucked out and did not get called on for some reason. I listened again to stories about drinking and pot smoking and sex with relatives, animals and more. I just kept thinking, what am I doing with these crazy people? Finally they told us to line up for bathroom and lunch. I noticed one of the door guys looking at me. I tried not to look back. I didn't want to get restrained, which is basically being sat on until they say you can leave. Lunch was peanut butter and jelly on white bread. And a glass of water. After lunch I was told I wasn't going to afternoon group. A level three took my leash and said that I had been selected as in need of individual counseling and I was brought to the main house. I was led upstairs to a small room, which was bare except for a desk and chair. And one of the door guys. Apparently counseling was done by graduates who had completed the program. I have to stop writing now. I was just told the hour is up and I have to make sure no one sees my real journal hidden in my MI journal.

Sometime in December 1985

I have not been able to write because I've had to re-write my moral inventory almost every night since what I shared wasn't good enough. They have been trying to make me cry, but I won't give them the satisfaction. At least I haven't peed my pants or been restrained. I just get yelled at. I was constipated for the first couple of weeks (I think it was weeks) because I didn't want to go with someone staring at me, but I finally gave in. I guess it is time to tell about how I got my regular journal back. The first time I was taken to counseling, it was with the door guy. His name is Dave. After I was led into the "counseling room" he locked the door sat on the one chair and told me to sit on the floor. What was I going to do? I sat on the floor. Then he looks at me with this sick smile, holds up my journal (how he got that I don't know) and says,

"I'll bet you'd like this." I didn't say anything. By this time I learned that the more you say the more you get abused. Part of the humbling process. Then he looks at me and says, "If you do something for me, I will do something for you." Then the next thing I know he is unzipping his pants. And takes his thing out and says, "You know what to do. I know all about your slutty ways." I didn't move. Then he says, "Do you really think you can play hard to get, you whore?" He grabbed my hair, pulled my head back and pinched my nostrils shut so I had to open my mouth. When he was finished he said, "Good girl," and patted me on the head like a dog. Welcome to counseling and I couldn't even go to the bathroom and brush my teeth. Then he said that since I held up my part of the bargain, he was going to give me my journal. He said that he would make sure that the on-duty level three night person wouldn't take it. But only if I did what he said. Then he told me how things really worked here. He told me that I needed to make up stories, the wilder the better, for my inventory and volunteer constantly to read them and cry and say how sorry I was for my bad behavior. That, he said, was the only way to get off level one. If I did exactly what he said, from now on and didn't tell anybody, I could be on level two in a matter of weeks. So that is what I have been doing. The group loves it. They "I love you, Devon" me to death. Hopefully, I will level up soon. Once I get to level two, I get tutoring and I get to have supervised contact with my Mom and Step Dad. I don't call her TW anymore, because that is druggie behavior. And I get to write in my journal as long as I go to counseling. I've gotten used to it. The quicker I get it over with the more time I get to hear about what really goes on in the program. Dave has made my life much better. At least I get to talk. I've stopped thinking about Tyler as much. Dave has helped me see that I was whoring around with Tyler and being a slut and I caused my problems because of that. And I've managed to not get restrained or sent to seclusion, even once. This girl Courtney did. She went crazy and said she wanted to leave.

They restrained her and wouldn't let her up, even to go to the bathroom. Then they led her to the seclusion room. I didn't see her for three days. When she got back from seclusion, she looked awful. And she confessed to all sorts of horrible things in group. She looked like a zombie. Dave said not to worry, that as long as I worked my program nothing like that would happen to me. He was going to protect me.

1986

Sometime during the first week of January

At least that is what I think it is. The days seem to blend together here. The holidays came and went. Level threes got to go home and spend Christmas and New Year's with their families. Level twos got to sing Christmas carols and help decorate the tree in the main house. I was still on level one so nothing was different for me. But they allowed us one supervised call to our parents for New Year's Day. It felt really weird speaking to my Mom. I didn't know what to say. She kept asking if I was OK and told me that she missed me, but that she knew my being here was for the best, and that I must graduate from the program. Dave was supervising my call so I couldn't say anything except how much I loved her and was sorry for hurting her and how grateful I was to be saved by the program. Dave said he would move me to level two after that. On level two I will get tutoring in the morning and more to eat. And more bathroom privileges. I will also get to go to family meeting once a month where we sit in a room with our parents on Friday nights and apologize for our behavior. Family meeting is where we level up. So we get to see when level twos become level threes and when level threes graduate and go home. On level two, we get a regular heated cabin to sleep in, with sheets and a blanket and a pillow. It has a sink and bathroom and we are allowed to go by ourselves. We still get locked in at night for our safety, and we still have to use the showers in the bathhouse once a week on Saturdays. They give us five minutes for showers. No blow drying of hair; it has to dry on its own. We also get to choose the color of our barrettes. I will finally get to read. Textbooks only, but, at least it's something. We don't get to listen to music until level three. I want to catch up in my school work. My school sent textbooks from my classes, but since all of us are working on different things, I will have to do my work by myself. The tutor is only there to help if I don't understand something. I guess I'll do the best I can. I will still go to afternoon and evening group, except for the afternoons I have counseling. Also on level two, we get to take hikes on Saturdays and Sundays instead of group. Oh, and no more leash!! That is the best part. But they want us to report every time someone breaks the rules. That is considered tough love, because once you are a level two you have shown that you can take more responsibility. And you have to prove you deserve it. This Friday is parent group. I will see my Mom and Chris for the first time since I got here. I hope they see how much I have changed. I also get regular clothes back and I can't wait for that! I am so sick of these sweats and canvas shoes. They suck in the snow. I have to make sure that I keep everything on my shelf perfectly folded and clean. But at least I don't have to wear the same clothes every week. I also get to choose a job for one afternoon a week. Level twos get a choice of helping in the kitchen/serving food, or laundry. Some newbies came today. This one guy refused to admit he had a drug problem. He swore he only tried pot once. The level three running the group got right in his face and told him he was lying, in denial and called him all kinds of nasty things. Then he spit on him. Right on his face. That's what they do to wake you up. You can't wipe it off either, you just have to sit there in your chair and take it. I only had it happen to me once and that was enough. Besides, Dave looks out for me so I haven't gotten the worst of it. And now he made sure that I'm moving up to level two. I still have to go for our "counseling" sessions, but he said as long as I do what is expected of me I'll be fine. I'm worried about somebody finding this journal and finding out, but he keeps telling me not to worry and that he will fix things. There is this one level two who is a bitch. Her name is Josephine and she loves getting people in trouble. I know she has it in for me, because I think she has a crush on Dave and has been watching when I go to counseling. She asked to escort me back and forth to counseling, and the office is letting her. She says she is just helping people work their program, but still… So many things happen here that seem bad on the outside, but we are told that people who work their program get out. I wonder who they hang out with though. It must be lonely because the program says that when you graduate and go home you can't be around any of your druggie friends or family members who use. I wonder if Chris is still drinking. Oh, and I keep hearing how what Chris did to me was my fault. I caused it and deserved it because of my behavior. I'm beginning to think it's true, otherwise why would I be here? When you graduate you have to belong to a 12-Step group and get signatures that you attend, or you have to come back here and start the program all over again. Unless you work for Rolling Hills like Dave. Then that is your service. Well that's it for today, "lights out" is soon and I still have to complete my moral inventory for tomorrow.

Four months later…May 27th, 1986

I am home now. I can't believe it. It feels so weird. I'm sleeping in my own room, in my own bed. No lock on the door. I am allowed to eat what I want, wear what I want. So many choices. I am not used to that. But I'm home. I guess I should write about why and what happened in the past four months. It's hard to talk about. It all feels like a bad dream, and in fact I still have nightmares every night. I wake up in a cold sweat and forget I am back home. It's just me and Mom. Chris is gone. Mom made him move out. He kept losing jobs because of his drinking and Mom got sick of paying all the bills. Plus, Rolling Hills told her for my sobriety and hers, he should not be in the house. I'm glad he's gone. After what he said to me in parents' group that Friday night, I hate him. Even if everything was all my fault.

I have a private tutor so that I can catch up on my work. Mom spoke to my guidance counselor and I can re-enter school in September as a junior if I successfully complete my work.

I won't be back in all honors classes because I've missed too much school. I am scared to go back to school. The program told me not to be around my former druggie friends. But Tyler is at college and Joni is in NYC. I haven't spoken to or heard from either of them. I wasn't allowed to contact anyone while I was in Rolling Hills. I am lucky to have this journal back. I'm glad they didn't destroy it after what happened.

It was bad enough that Josephine read it. Especially after what happened. They fired Dave, but still blamed me. I don't know if I can tell about what happened. I have tried to block it out. The past four months are a blur, but it keeps coming back in nightmares. Mom is worried about me. She says I'm different. She thinks I'm afraid of everything and keeps telling me I don't have to ask permission to go to the bathroom, or to eat. She's been taking me to her 12-Step program meetings. That's pretty much the only time I go out. I get my sheet signed because I don't want to get sent back to that place. I haven't smoked pot either since I've been home. Where would I get it anyway? Mom drug tests me, too. I have to pee in a cup once a week. I don't care, I know I'm clean. My sweet 16 birthday happened while I was still in Rolling Hills, so Mom wants to celebrate with me now that I'm home. She thinks we should at least go out to dinner. But I am just grateful to be home. The outside world seems so scary to me. I don't know how to act anymore. So I don't go anywhere except meetings. People accept me there and don't think I'm weird. The people there are nice, but mostly old. No people my age. I haven't gotten a sponsor yet. I don't share either, and nobody makes me. They say the only requirement to attend is a desire to be sober. Which I have.

Part of me wants to write about what happened, even though I deserved it and am a bad person. But I doubt anyone will believe what happens there at Rolling Hills. And what am I going to tell people when I go back to school? How do I explain where I've been? Mom says to just say I was in a private school. Which is true, but everybody probably knows

I was in rehab. My counselor knows. I have to go a special meeting with him before school starts. I wish I never made any of the bad choices I made. I wish I could start all over again and be someone else. But I can't. I am trying to make amends to Mom. For being a bad person, hurting her and making her spend all that money to make me a good person again. I tell her that over and over, but it doesn't make me feel any better and she just starts crying. She said she's worried about me. But then why did she take me home? I mean, I'm not complaining, I'm glad she did, but I was back on level one, I didn't even get to level up to two like Dave promised. Nobody gets to graduate from level one. All I know is one day I got called down to the main building. My Mom was there and we had a meeting with an administration person and my Mom said she was taking me home. The admin person pleaded with her not to, and said I would die and start using again and that I needed to finish the program. But my Mom told them that the insurance was no longer paying and it was too expensive. Then the admin person told her to get a second mortgage and that she was being a bad mother by not taking care of me. Then Mom did something I have never seen her do. She told them no. She said enough was enough, and that she thought that they made me worse. She said she was taking me home, that she was not going to discuss it anymore, and then she said, "Come on Devon, it's time to leave." They gave me my personal things, including my journal, which they thought they had confiscated but didn't, and we walked out the door. On the way home, she kept apologizing and saying she was sorry for putting me there, that it was all Chris' idea. That's when I found out she threw him out and was getting divorced. She keeps trying to get me to talk about what happened. She keeps apologizing for what Chris said and what happened at the family group meeting. I just want to forget it. It's too painful to talk about and I keep trying to block it out, but then the nightmares come. She wants me to go to a therapist, but then I would have to talk about what happened and have to listen to another person tell me what a defective person I am. I just want to be left alone. Actually, I don't feel much of anything. I feel numb. Like I am just going through the motions of life. Maybe someday I'll feel normal again. I wonder what it's like to be a normal 16-year-old? Other kids are getting ready for the end of the school year and looking for jobs for the summer. I'll be working with the tutor and going to 12-Step meetings. Part of me doesn't want to go back to school at all. I just don't want to deal with that. But then I'm running away from my responsibility. Mom says I have to start thinking about college. She says that's why it is so important that I catch up with the tutor. I used to want to go to college. I don't know what I want anymore. Most of the time I don't even know what I feel.

July 5th, 1986

Mom took me to the shore yesterday for the holiday. We walked along the boardwalk and ate ice cream. I saw a bunch of kids my age hiding under the boardwalk getting high and drinking beer. That used to be me. I don't know any kids like me anymore. I wonder what happens to the people who graduate the program. The only ones I know were still involved at Rolling Hills. Except Dave. He got fired and who knows where he is now. Most of the kids who got to level three ended up moving nearby and working for the program either full or part time as part of their recovery and service. They said this was what they needed to do to stay alive and sober. So what do they do, stay in Deposit, NY, for the rest of their lives? The program administrator keeps calling Mom and offering discounts to bring me back. Thank God she's said no. She told them she is my mother and she makes the decisions. I hope she doesn't send me back. I don't care if my life is boring and weird. I'm not using and that's what's important. But school starts in less than two months so every-thing will change then. I'll have to get used to being around other kids, and kids who use. I guess if I just come right home after school it won't matter. I can just do my work and come home and go to meetings and do my homework. Mom goes on weekends now, too, so I can go every day. I still don't have a sponsor but I'm trying to work my steps. I know I am powerless and in danger of relapse any day, but I'm doing my best to stay away from people and places that will trigger me. Which is why I'm nervous about school. Oh, and Mom keeps talking about taking me to see a therapist. She thinks I'm depressed or something. She said she found someone in town who works with teens. She thinks I'm depressed because of all the change in my life and because Gram died. I guess I'm defective and need to be fixed. I don't know. I don't even know who I am anymore.

July 31st, 1986

I took a walk into town to get some groceries for the house. Other than going to the library for my tutoring sessions, and going to meetings, I'm still pretty much in the house. Mom wants me to go to the pool at least, but I just haven't been in the mood. I walked past the record store but didn't go in because I'm not supposed to listen to druggie music and the only music Rolling Hills said was OK was the oldies station. We have an oldies station here in town that is on AM radio so I listen to that. All my albums just sit there gathering dust. I keep being afraid that if I listen to them Mom will send me back to that place, which is silly because she says she won't. I've kind of gotten used to oldies. The Shirelles and Bobby Darin are my new best friends. So, anyway, when I walked past the record store, Tyler was working there. I have not seen him since I went away. I was going to just walk by, but he saw me and called me over. When I didn't come in he ran out and grabbed me! "Hey Devon, where have you been? I tried calling you and your Mom said you went away to private school. Why didn't you call or write to me? What the fuck?" I looked at him and said what Rolling Hills told us to say if we ended up seeing our old druggie friends. "I'm sorry Tyler, but I can't hang out with you anymore." I started to walk away, but he grabbed my arm, and yelled at me, "That's it, that's all you are going to say? I don't hear from you for months and that's what you say? Fuck you, Devon!" And then he stormed back into the store. Guess I won't be walking by there again. I guess I'll have to walk an extra mile to the Quik Check from now on so I don't run into him. At least he's no longer at the high school. I don't have to worry about seeing him there. My re-orientation meeting with guidance is in three weeks. I have a new guidance counselor. It's a man named Mr. Frederick. I've seen him before but never talked with him. I haven't been in that high school since last fall. That feels like years, not months. It is going to feel really weird to go back. At least I didn't get left back and recovered my credits. There are some benefits to having nothing to do. I got all my work made up and my summer reading done as well. Except now I'm bored. I've been taking books out of the library to read, but that gets old. Mom wants me to go to aerobics with her. She's on this new health kick. I am so bored I may actually go. Besides, the house is spotless because all I do is clean. And listen to the oldies station. Oh, and she scheduled an appointment with the therapist. Her name is Dr. Fine(!) and her office is in one of the Victorian houses by the college. The first session is going to be with me and Mom. I guess I have to go. I don't want to talk about my feelings or what happened. I just want to go on with my life, but if it's a choice between going to another rehab or this, I'll take this. The nightmares are less frequent now, but I still get them. Apparently, I yell in my sleep and that freaks Mom out. She seems to be doing pretty well without Chris. I found out that she got a restraining order on him because he threatened to kill her one night when he was drunk. What an asshole. But I already knew that. I am glad he's out of our lives. Mom seems to be OK with being single now. She goes out sometimes with her girlfriends on weekend nights and she's still sober so I give her credit for that. She is trying so hard to be nice to me. I told her not to worry. I'm just grateful to be home. At least she's not blaming me for what happened with Dave. We never talk about it, but it is always there in the back of my mind, ready to come out in a nightmare.

August 15th, 1986

I had my first appointment with Dr. Fine. First she met with my Mom and me together. My Mom did most of the talking. She talked about how guilty she felt that she got married too soon after she came back in my life, and how she tried her best to be a good mother and listened too much to Chris and that is how I ended up at Rolling Hills. Then she told Dr. Fine about me having sex with Dave! I thought I was going to die! She said that she blamed herself and the program. That's news to me, I knew she thought the program made me worse but she never said it was her fault. But she didn't tell the whole story because she started to cry, didn't finish and made it all about her. She also didn't tell about what happened at the parent meeting with me. She brought it up, but Dr. Fine said if we chose to work with her, it would be up to me to decide when I wanted to reveal any details. Dr. Fine said it was obvious that both of us had been through a very tough time. Then Mom started to cry again and said she never wanted me to go through what she went through with Gramps, and told Dr. Fine that Gramps raped her, repeatedly from the age of 13 until she left home. He would come to her room at night, when he was drunk and Gram was asleep. I was in shock. But after hearing that, things started to make sense. Now I understood why she left home and why Gram made me put that lock on the door. Dave didn't rape me, it was just oral sex. But it still made me feel dirty. And now I hate Gramps. I am glad he's dead. But what about Gram? Why didn't she do anything? How could she let that just happen? Especially if she knew? Why would she do that? I can't get those questions out of my head. And why didn't Mom do anything when I got called out at the family meeting that night at Rolling Hills? Why did she let Chris say the awful things he said to me? I thought since all she did was sit there and cry that everything that happened was my fault and that she thought that too. I've been trying to block it out, but now it keeps coming up in my head. But let me finish about the session first. So, after Mom finally stopped crying, Dr. Fine explained how she worked. She said that when she works with teens, she meets with them individually for one session and with the family for a family session since family issues often contribute to teen behavior, and that improving communication between me and my Mom would be important, as well as understanding the family behaviors that get passed down over generations, especially when abuse and alcohol are involved. She explained that she only works individually with teens if the teenager wants to be in treatment, and that if so, sessions are confidential unless the teen expresses the desire to hurt her/himself or others, such as in the case of suicide or if a teen threatens to kill someone! I can't see myself doing that, but OK, I guess some people do. Dr. Fine also said that she is mandated by law to tell child services if I report any abuse. She said that if a safety-related concern comes up in an individual session, then she would discuss that with me first and then have a session with me and my Mom to discuss it and decide on the next steps. She explained that individual sessions were for me to discuss what I wanted to discuss and that if I chose to work with her, she and I would develop goals and a treatment plan together. Dr. Fine also told Mom that it was very important for her (Mom) to be patient with the process, and not force me to talk about anything that happened before that was painful (unless there was a current safety issue, like suicide or something like that). She suggested that Mom get her own therapist to talk to as well. I don't think Mom liked that idea. She said she goes to meetings and that is enough, but that she will go to the family sessions for me.

You know, I liked Dr. Fine. She is very easy to talk to and made me feel comfortable right away. She's about the same age as Mom, but looks older because her hair is a bit gray. It is shoulder-length and curly and she was wearing one of those long flowy dresses that middle-aged women like to wear. There were diplomas on the wall. She went to Skidmore College and Rutgers, the State University of New Jersey, for her Psy.D. I didn't even know that was a degree. Apparently it is a new kind of doctorate for people who want to practice psychology, as opposed to teaching or research. I just thought therapists were therapists. At Rolling Hills all you needed to do to be a counselor was graduate. And look what happened to me. But, I'll get to that…so Dr. Fine also told us that we both needed to make a commitment to be sober for the duration of treatment or it would not be effective. She explained that some issues might be painful to discuss, but that using or drinking to avoid them would not be helpful. That part didn't surprise me. What did surprise me was what she said after that. Dr. Fine explained that using was not bad in and of itself, that it is just one way of coping with pain, or avoiding boredom or unpleasant feelings. She said the purpose of therapy was to find healthy ways for coping with emotions, so that I would not want or need to use drugs. That was interesting because Rolling Hills just told us it was bad, period, and would destroy our life and that we were powerless over it. They never said it was just a behavior or way to cope. And they never told us how to cope with difficult emotions. They just told us we were supposed to take responsibility and deal with them ourselves, and we had to accept responsibility for everything that happened to us, because our druggie behavior caused it. We were not allowed to blame anyone else except when we were calling out someone in group. And that was considered an intervention called "tough love."

Anyway, I agreed to see Dr. Fine. I like her. She actually listens and does not judge. I've never met an adult like her. She also treats me with respect, not like some dumb kid. She loves that I journal and said to keep it up, that it was a good way to express my emotions and that it was private and for my eyes only (she gave my mother a look when she said that). I really liked that. Eventually, I will tell about what happened in family group that Friday night in Rolling Hills, but not yet. When I try to write about it I get anxious and can't breathe. I agreed to see Dr. Fine individually, and Mom agreed to the family sessions, but not to finding her own therapist. Maybe she'll change her mind, but I doubt it.

August 22nd, 1986

I had my first individual session with Dr. Fine yesterday. It was not what I expected at all. The first thing she asked me was to think about three things I wanted to change in my life and how I wanted them to be different. I didn't know how to respond at first. No adult (or person my age even) had ever asked me that. It made me realize that I've spent my life doing what I think other people want me to do. After my Mom came back into my life, Kyle broke up with me and Gramps and then Gram died, I decided that what I want doesn't matter because nothing and nobody lasts. When I met Joni and Tyler I was so happy to have friends that I just did whatever they wanted to do because I was getting out of my house and having fun. Or at least what I thought was fun. You know, when I think about it, smoking and drinking were just things I did while spending time with them. I had fun because it brought us together. Especially with Tyler. Now that I look back on it, I was doing things for him to make him happy and not thinking if those things would make me happy. I wanted to be with him so much that my happiness was not important, being with him was. Neither he nor Joni ever wanted to hear about my feelings or talk to me about Gram's death, so I just buried those feelings away and thought if I didn't think about bad things they wouldn't bother me. But bad things happened anyway. Rolling Hills said drugs ruined my relationships. I don't think that is totally true. Drugs became a focus of my relationships because they happened to be there and part of the entertainment. I didn't do them specifically to do them, well at least not until I realized that pot helped calm me down. So, anyway, the only answer I could come up with for Dr. Fine was that I wanted to be a normal kid, who lives at home, has friends and goes to school like other kids. Because that is what I want. I'm sick of having a weird family that is not like other people's families and I hate that when I finally made friends and had a boyfriend I got sent away. And not just sent away, but sent to that horrible place. So, I told her I just wanted to be a normal kid. Then she asked me what things I most enjoyed, things that when I did them made me lose track of time because I liked them so much. I had to think a long time about that because I have not felt passionate about anything for a long time. And then I realized that I used to be passionate about guitar playing and music. Somehow, that went away. And when Dr. Fine asked me when I last remembered feeling passionate about guitar, that's when I thought of Kyle. And I realized that I stopped playing guitar because it reminded me of Kyle and made me feel sad that we broke up because I had to move. And then it made me angry at Mom again for taking me away from Gram and my life in Warwick. And mad at Julia for taking Kyle away from me. And mad at Kyle for acting like all he wanted was sex. So, I told Dr. Fine that and she didn't tell me I was a bad person or selfish for thinking that (which is what Rolling Hills would have said). Instead, she told me that she understood why I would have those feelings and that anyone in my situation would have those feelings. That was a surprise to me. Nobody ever told me that my feelings were normal before. It felt really good and almost made me cry. Then she asked me what I thought it would be like if I could separate out my guitar playing from Kyle and my Mom. That got me thinking again but I had no answer. She looked at me and said, "Devon, what do you think it would be like if you took back your passion for guitar and made it yours without associating it with Kyle or your mother?" It made me realize that guitar playing belonged to me and only me. I could decide to play to make myself happy and why shouldn't I play guitar if it makes me happy? And you know what? For the first time in years, I took out my guitar today and played a few chords. It felt really good. I don't remember the songs I wrote in the past, but it felt good to play again even if it was just chords. I can't wait to tell her the next time I see her! My next session is the family session, in a couple of days. That's where I meet with Dr. Fine and my Mom to talk to each other about more than the weather or 12-Step stuff. We are going to create a genogram, which is a fancy word for a family tree and take a look at the people in our family. It's funny, I don't know much about my family, even my mother's side. I know my mother had a younger brother who died when she was young, but that was something that no one ever talked about. Ever. So I don't know how he died or anything about him. I wonder if we'll talk about that? There are so many family secrets that are coming out. Like about Mom and Gramps. That still creeps me out. How could he do that to her? And why? It's like part of me wants to know and the other part is afraid to know. What else weird did my family do? I heard a lot of weird stories at Rolling Hills, but Dave said most people made them up to level up so I have no idea if my family is weird or not. Do other kids at school have parents with alcohol problems and who do sick things? It's not like anybody is going to talk about it at a normal school. And with school starting soon I feel nervous. Dr. Fine just said that if anyone asks where I was to just say my Mom and her ex-husband sent me away to private school and leave it at that. Which is true. But I got so used to telling long, crazy, stories at Rolling Hills for fear of being called in denial or a liar that I'm afraid no one will believe me and they'll bother me until I tell them more. At Rolling Hills, the worst thing you could do was not talk about how weird you were. You were not allowed to be normal or you wouldn't be there in the first place. At least that's what the group leaders said. After all, they were level threes or graduates. I am really starting to realize what a crazy place that was. Dr. Fine told me I don't have to listen to Rolling Hills' preaching anymore. And that's what it felt like. Preaching. Like I was part of some demented church. You know, it feels good to get this out on paper. It feels good to say what I really think.

August 27th, 1986

I had my first family session with Mom and Dr. Fine. As promised, we did the genogram of the family. I was at the bottom with a line sticking out of a circle that said Devon. The line pointed upward and connected to a horizontal line with two lines pointing up, where they connected to a circle on the left called Devon's father with a question mark, and on the right side connected to a circle that said Paula Anderson Downing. A horizontal line connected her to a circle with a big X, her brother's name (Patrick) and his year of death. Then a line that came out of the Paula circle pointed up and had a horizontal line connected to two vertical lines on either side with circles with Gramps on the left and Gram on the right and the dates they died. Dr. Fine said we would start with these people first and then add more circles (people) from previous generations if needed. I guess she figured we had enough craziness to talk about with just us. She didn't say that though. When she finished with the diagram, she asked about my father, the question mark. I said I had no idea who he was. Mom said she had no idea who he was either, that he could be one of several people she slept with at Woodstock and doesn't remember because she was tripping the whole time. Dr. Fine asked if I had ever asked about or wondered who my father was. I said, "Of course, but how would I find out?" She told us that there is a registry that adults and adult children can sign up for that helps locate and reunite birth parents with their children. But both parties have to agree and the child has to be the age of consent, which is 18. So, while I'm not old enough now, this is something I can do later, and could be helpful in terms of my medical history. I never thought of that. I just always wondered who my father was, what he looked like and what he does. I never really considered his health as something that would affect me. What if he is really sick, or dead? Part of me wishes I was 18 right now so I could find out (assuming he wanted to meet me) and part of me doesn't think I can deal with another parent. Mom is enough to deal with and Chris is finally out of the house. I didn't say that, but Dr. Fine also asked Mom about her ongoing divorce from Chris and added his circle to the other side of the Paula circle with his name and birthdate, wrote married with that date, and then wrote "undergoing divorce (current)." Dr. Fine asked how each of our relationships were with Chris. Mom spoke first on that one. She started to cry and say how wonderful he was at first and how he was so good to her and that they finally found her dream house and were going to live happily ever after with me. But then, she said, I started rebelling and breaking rules and Chris lost his job and started drinking and that Chris resented me and would complain about me all the time, and he started losing jobs and getting angry and abusive when he was drunk. Mom said she was at her wits' end when he told her about the Rolling Hills program. Chris had heard about it from some friend at one of his jobs, and the friend said it cured his son, who was now a straight A student who had a part time job and went to AA meetings instead of parties with his former druggie friends. Mom told Dr. Fine that she thought sending me away would both help me get back to my former self and give her time to work on her marriage, but things didn't work out quite the way she expected. She had doubts about leaving me at Rolling Hills, especially because there was no contact with parents during level one, which could be a month or longer. She said she had to sign a 50-page parent agreement all about how the program worked. (I wonder how much they told her; I saw a brochure of the place and I swear it looked like a country club for kids, not the place I was in). She had regular phone contact with them where they told her about my progress (or lack of) and how it was vital to keep me there at least until I graduate, or I would progress in my addiction and die. They kept telling her that they would fix me so that I was her daughter again – obedient, kind and compliant. She told Dr. Fine that she had a nagging voice telling her something didn't seem right, after all, shouldn't she be able to visit and spend time alone with her child? But Chris told her that spoiling me and being too lenient was what contributed to me being a problem child. Mom told Dr. Fine that he convinced her that I was just a spoiled brat who needed to be taught a lesson. Mom said she loved Chris and that he was her dream man so she went along with him, even though he was becoming more and more verbally abusive to her and less reliable with working, and he was drinking more. Mom said she started going to Al-Anon meetings, which really helped her and she was able to detach from Chris when he was drinking. Until the night he threatened to kill her. (I guess that's when she finally woke up.) After she got the restraining order and left, she found out he had been stealing money from her inheritance, and that her savings were eroding. So, when the insurance company stopped paying for Rolling Hills she put her foot down. She apologized again to me, in front of Dr. Fine, there were more tears, etc. etc. Dr. Fine asked how I felt about Chris being out of our lives now. I told her I couldn't be happier, that I hated him and never wanted to see him again. Then I looked at my Mom and said, "Especially after the way he treated me at the family meeting." Then I started to hyperventilate and Dr. Fine suggested that we give me a moment to take some deep breaths and relax and that we did not need to discuss Chris right now or the family meeting incident if I was not ready. I appreciated that because I could tell Mom was going to barrel right on ahead and talk about how she felt and I would get lost in the background as usual. Anyway, by that time the session was almost over, so Dr. Fine said that I could talk about my feelings with her privately if I chose. I don't feel ready yet, but maybe someday. When it's not so painful and overwhelming. When I can talk about it and breathe. I could tell Mom was disappointed. She wants this process to be over as soon as possible. I am surprised to say this, but I'm not sure I do. I like seeing Dr. Fine. She helps me to make sense of the craziness of the people around me and doesn't treat me like I'm the crazy one. In our next private session she's going to teach me something called "progressive muscle relaxation," which is a meditation technique that helps you to relax and feel "grounded." I think that sounds kind of cool. She wants to teach me ways to relax that are healthy, legal and that I can use in everyday life. I like that. I like the thought of being in control of my emotions without someone telling me what to do or what to feel. It makes me feel better; happier in a way. Dr. Fine also told both of us how she really likes that I am journaling after sessions and that writing about my thoughts and feelings is an excellent coping strategy. She said it's teaching me how to reflect on my actions and behaviors as well as my thoughts and it is teaching me to think about how I want to handle things in the future.

September 4th, 1986

Today was the first day of school. It was really hot. I wish they had air-conditioning in that place. It felt really strange and uncomfortable to be back there. I felt like everyone was staring at me, even the teachers. It was almost like people were trying so hard to act like nothing happened, which is total bullshit. I ran into some kids I knew, but most of the kids in my classes I did not know. Except for Honors English. But even that class had a lot of new kids I had never met before. One of the kids stood out in a sea of mullet-heads. He was wearing a brightly colored tie-dyed shirt and had long straggly hair that he wore in a ponytail. I took my seat next to him, and he smiled at me and said, "Hi." I said, "Hi" back and that was the extent of our conversation.

When I met with my guidance counselor last week to go over my schedule and get reoriented he assured me that all my teachers were aware of what I had been through and were told not to talk to me about it or let other kids talk to me about it. What are the teachers supposed to do? Tape kids' mouths shut? But at least nobody, teacher or otherwise, asked me. I did get some stares though. Now I'm known as that kid that got sent away to rehab/private school. I feel like I have a sign on me that says, "I am not normal." I know that's in my head and Dr. Fine is working on it with me. I've been doing the relaxation exercises she taught me, but they never work as well by myself as they do in her office when she does the guided meditation in real time. She has this very comfortable couch I sit on and I really do feel relaxed and calm after the 15-minute meditation is over. She made a tape recording of it so that I can listen and practice at home. But here's what happens, I go in my room and lie down. Then I put on my Walkman to listen to the tape. Usually I am able to focus on relaxing my head and neck muscles. Then when we get to shoulders, my mind starts to wander. Hmmm…it starts thinking…Did I get that homework assignment handed in on time? I wonder what is going to happen at the assembly tomorrow? That boy who sits next to me in English is really cool. And before I know it I forget that there's a voice in my ears that is supposed to help me relax, because I've drowned it out in favor of the voices in my head. Dr. Fine told me that happens in the beginning and that when I catch myself doing it I should just gently remind myself to focus back on the tape, and that it's OK even to start it over and try again. So I do that, except now 30 minutes have gone by and sure enough Mom is yelling from downstairs. "Devon, come down now, it's time to set the table and wash the salad greens for dinner." Zen feeling gone. I'm going to have to try this again when she's not home.

September 15th, 1986

So, I have the cool English teacher again. He's not running the Poetry Club anymore because there was not enough interest, but he runs an Acoustic Guitar Club for students that meets during lunch period on Thursday. Any of his students can bring their acoustic guitars to school and play and sing songs in his classroom during club time. And he also stays until 4 p.m. every day for people who want to hang out in his classroom after school and jam together. He lets them keep their guitars in a closet in the back of the room during the school day. Kids just drop them off before homeroom. The kid I sit next to in English class, Justin, is one of the guitar players. Justin is different from other kids I've met. He's a Deadhead, but he doesn't smoke pot because he also had to go to rehab and has to be sober because if he fails a drug test he gets kicked out of school. He went to this fancy-schmancy private hospital rehab in Montclair. Where rich kids go. It was nothing like Rolling Hills. They had group and counseling, but they also had school after the first month, and family therapy and individual therapy and AA meetings right at the hospital. They did all these different recreational activities like ropes courses and canoeing at Round Valley State Park. The trips were not until you earned them, though. They had a points system, but it seems like it was pretty easy to get points, not like Rolling Hills. And he said the kids were nice. He met his girlfriend there. Now he goes to AA meetings in Long Valley, which is just over Schooley's Mountain from Hacketts-town. His girlfriend lives in the next town over from there, Chester. He invited me to come with them to a meeting this Wednesday and I am going to go. I think it's cool that kids my age go to this meeting. The ones I've been going to are just a bunch of old people. They're nice to me and all, but they're old and I don't feel like I can relate to them and their job stress and kid stress and all that. I'm also going to start going to the Acoustic Guitar Club on Thursdays. I'm a bit nervous about playing in front of people, but if I know what chords to play I'm good. Well, there goes Mom yelling about making salad. So, time to chop vegetables and spin greens. Maybe I can try meditation tonight before bed. She probably won't interrupt me then. I think.

October 1st, 1986

I went to the meeting Justin goes to in Long Valley. Mom drove me and picked me up. She's been nicer lately. I think she feels really guilty about what happened at Rolling Hills. I haven't talked about that night or what happened with Dave with Dr. Fine yet. She isn't pushing me either. She said it's fine to move at my own pace and we're just working on identifying what my interests and goals are and working on ways to help me relax. I'm getting better at the relaxation meditation. I brought up in family session that I need time without interruption to practice it and Mom has been trying to be more respectful. I'm still kind of freaked out over what Mom revealed in family sessions so far. First about Gramps…and then about my uncle. His name was Patrick and he died when he got hit by a car. He was riding his bike in the street. Mom was supposed to be watching him, but she was looking the other way and bam, a car comes out of nowhere and hits him before she could do anything. One minute he was riding, the next he was lying in the street dead. She still blames herself for the accident. The driver of the car was an old man who felt terrible and called an ambulance. Mom says what happened next was a blur, but she ran home to tell Gram and Gramps (she just left him in the street?) and when the ambulance came and took him to the hospital he was pronounced dead. Mom says that after Patrick died was when Gramps really started to drink. Before that Gramps was just a workaholic. And then after he started drinking was when the abuse started. Mom says she felt like she deserved it because she killed her brother. I don't think she was responsible; she was just a kid herself and why weren't Gram and Gramps watching him? Gram used to watch me like a hawk. All the time. Maybe that's why. Maybe she felt guilty about Uncle Patrick. And why did Gram say Gramps had demons about the war? Why didn't she just tell me the real reason? These family sessions are really depressing. So many secrets, and sad ones, too. I wish I could just remember Gram and Gramps the way I thought they were when I was a kid. But, as painful as it is, hearing all of this is helping me understand why Mom is the way she is. Now I'm starting to see that she has been trying to get her life together and do the right thing. She just seems to have gotten fucked over by men. I see now that's how she ended up with Chris. I hope she has learned something and that the next man she gets involved with is a nicer person. I have mixed feelings about her now; I'm still angry with her, but I kind of feel bad for her too. She has not had an easy life. Anyway, about the meeting. I actually liked it. There are other kids my age, and I feel like I can relate to them. Most are there because they have to be in order to stay in school and graduate, but they seem to be getting something out of the meetings, even if it is just friends to talk to. I took down some phone numbers because we're supposed to make three calls a night so we don't "isolate." So far I've made one. To Justin, because I feel most comfortable with him. It's interesting because I don't like him as more than a friend, but I just feel relaxed around him. He is so laid back and accepting. I asked him what it is like to be a Deadhead and not do drugs. He said that he wasn't into the Dead because of drugs. Listening to and following the Dead was about their music, not an excuse to do drugs. He thinks Jerry Garcia is God. Well, not really, but pretty close to it. He goes to concerts whenever they come to Giants stadium or the Garden. He's trying to get something called "taper's tickets" where they let you stay in the special section with microphones and tape the show. He has a gazillion Dead tapes from shows going back to the '70s. He's going to make some for me to listen to. I kind of like the stuff from *Workingman's Dead* and *American Beauty* and have been practicing the songs on my guitar, and play them when we play them in Acoustic Guitar Club, but I'm not sure about the live stuff. It sounds kind of sloppy and the tapes are not always good quality, but Deadheads don't care. They think if Jerry comes on stage and farts it's awesome. And not because they're tripping or high. It's almost like a religion to them. But, you know what, I'm cool with that because the Deadheads I've met are really nice people. I was afraid they were going to give me shit for not getting high (Rolling Hills warned us about that), but they're not like that at all. Most of the ones I know are in AA anyway, so they're sober. I met some other kids at the AA meeting (including Justin's girlfriend – her name is Jessie) and they're cool. Justin says he's not going to be sober forever, just until college so he can graduate high school and get into a good college. He wants to be a marine biologist. I think that's cool. He told me that he has an aquarium in his room, with all sorts of exotic fish. I'm going to go to a Dead show with Justin and Jessie when the Dead comes around. They have been talking about the coma Jerry was in and that they're glad he survived. He was in a diabetic coma for a week, but came out of it. Supposedly the Dead are going back into the studio to record a new album early next year, so Justin thinks they'll tour next summer. It's going to be weird for me to be around all those kids who get high. Also, sitting in the taper seats will be strange, because I just don't get what is so magical about the Dead and I still don't get the whole Jerry Garcia thing. Maybe I just have to see them live. I really like Jessie. She is this really thin and tall girl with light blue eyes and long curly hair that she just lets grow wild. I think that's cool; it makes her stand out from the hair-mousse crowd. My own hair is just boring. I don't do anything to it but let it dry by itself, and it's straight. Jessie told me she thinks it's beautiful. Isn't it funny how girls always want what they don't have, like straight hair if you have curly and vice versa. Anyway, Jessie wears these long hippie skirts and ankle bracelets. She is like a throwback to Woodstock. When I told her my Mom went to Woodstock, she got all excited and now she really wants to meet my Mom. She said the Dead played at Woodstock along with lots of other cool bands she likes. I didn't think there were any hippies left, especially my age, but Deadheads are like people left back in time. Even though I'm not crazy about the music, they are literally the nicest people I've met in a long time. Jessie is really into art and wants to go to college for it. She said she wants to go to a Liberal Arts school that has a good art program, because unless she gets famous and sells a lot of her work she'll probably end up having to teach to make money. I think it is so cool that she already knows what she wants to do. And here's a surprise… the Deadhead kids actually care about grades and careers and stuff. They want to go to college and not just to party (well, at least the sober ones). At Rolling Hills they told us that all kids who do (or even did) drugs, even just marijuana, are druggie losers who end up living on the street. That is not what these kids are like at all. I'm starting to think that I was brain-washed by Rolling Hills. I hate when people stereotype other people. Like all the cliques in high school. The jocks don't hang out with the metal heads and the band kids don't hang out with anyone but themselves. It's like everyone in high school is stuck in their own little bubble. What I like about Jessie and Justin is that they like you for who you are, they don't expect you to be like them or act a certain way. So, why is it bad for me to hang out with them because they used to do drugs? They aren't trying to make me do them. They really don't care if people do them or not. It's just not important to them. You know, I think adults just create these ideas about kids, but it's like they don't even know who kids are. It's like we're another species. Except Dr. Fine. I really think she gets it. She's the only adult I know who just listens and helps me figure out what I want and what I think will be best for me, not just for the moment, but for when I'm older, too. She gets me thinking about my future. We've been talking about college and whether I want to go. I am starting to think I do. I really like English and writing so she has encouraged me to meet with my guidance counselor to start thinking about programs. The PSATs are in March and even though they're just practice, if you do well you qualify for a merit scholarship. All four-year colleges require the SATs (or something called the ACTs) and the good ones only take people with high scores. There's always community college, but those are only two-year programs so you have to transfer to a four-year college unless you get some kind of technical degree. It feels kind of overwhelming to me. Some of the honor students are already going with their parents to look at schools! How do they even know where they want to go? I think it would be kind of cool to go to a city school, like NYU or maybe BU. I don't want to go to a school in the middle of nowhere with fraternities and sororities because there is nothing to do but go to parties and drink. Jessie is thinking about BU because they have a good Fine Arts and Liberal Arts program. BU is very expensive, but Jessie's family has a lot of money. Her father is a doctor and her mother is a lawyer. Well, just thinking about all the choices makes me hyperventilate. But not like when I'm having a flashback to Rolling Hills or about Dave. Some of the boys in Acoustic Guitar Club have been trying to talk to me and I just don't want to deal with them. The only boy I feel comfortable around right now is Justin. He treats me with respect, as a friend, and would never hit on me because he loves Jessie. And, even if I was attracted to him (which I am not) I would never do that to Jessie. I really like her and want to hang out with her more. It's too bad we go to different schools. But Mom said I can invite them over for dinner on a weekend, and since Jessie's been dying to meet my Mom and ask her about Woodstock, I'll probably have them over soon. Jessie also wants me to come hang out with her at her house and I definitely want to do that.

October 15th, 1986

Well, I did it. I told Dr. Fine what happened that night at Rolling Hills. How Josephine ratted me out and told everyone about me and Dave, and then I told her what happened at the family meeting. I did it in family session, not my individual session. I wanted my Mom to hear how I felt. It made her cry again, but the whole point of family sessions is to communicate, and communicate I did. It opened up a whole can of worms, but first things first. Now that I talked about what happened, Dr. Fine has encouraged me to write about my feelings about it, so write I will. She says that will help me heal. Here's what happened. After the phone call with Mom that I had to make in front of Dave, everything went to hell. I was supposed to level up at the Friday night parent meeting. But Josephine found my diary. She was assigned to do a full bunk check to make sure all of our stuff was neat and our beds were made and I didn't realize that they check underneath everything. She found my diary. And then, the next day at morning group, she read it aloud to everyone. She read the parts about being at Rolling Hills and how I was having oral sex with Dave in counseling. And the worst part was that Dave was one of the door watchers that day. Everyone ganged up on me. They made me sit in a chair, in the middle of all of them and each of them walked by me, called me a liar and a whore. And spit on me. They had Dave hold me down on the chair so I couldn't move. I just sat there with the spit on my face and cried. Dave did nothing to defend me like he promised. He acted just like the rest of them. Then as a punishment they made me take off my clothes and walk around in my underwear all day. Wherever I went. People would point at me and laugh and say, "Look at the whore!" And of course, my diary was taken away. That day seemed to last forever. I told everyone how sorry I was and what a loser I was and blah, blah, blah, and when the day was over everyone told me they loved me and that now I could finally recover. And of course, I did not level up at the Friday night meeting. The administration decided that they needed to fire Dave because they didn't want what happened getting out to the public, but it got brought up at the parent meeting. They humiliated me there too, in front of everyone, parents and all. They had me sit up front (but in my clothes, thank God) and Josephine told all the parents what I did (yes, what I did, because they said I came on to Dave, and that he was gone because they were trying to protect him from me). Then they invited my parents to speak. Mom didn't say anything, she just cried. But Chris did. He yelled at me for 10 minutes straight, telling me what a horrible person I was, how he was ashamed to be my father (which he is not), how all I do is ruin people's lives and on and on until I was crying, too. All the other parents just looked at me and shook their heads. One actually asked if her son was safe from me. The rest is a blur. I just blocked it out and I don't even remember what it was like there after that. All I remember is my Mom taking me home. When I was finished telling my story, Dr. Fine, who is usually very calm, looked extremely upset. She told me and my Mom that what Rolling Hills and Dave did to me was sexual and emotional abuse. She said that I had nothing to be ashamed of and that I was a victim of a sick system and that what Chris did was wrong. Then she asked if we remembered what she had told us at the beginning of treatment, that what was said was confidential and that there were only certain things that did not fall under the confidentiality umbrella. She explained that as a psychologist she was mandated by law to report any disclosures of abuse. She said that we needed to report Rolling Hills and Dave to the authorities and that we could do it together from her office. I was like, report this? I have to tell people what happened? I did not want to do that, but she explained that it was for my safety and the protection of others, and that Rolling Hills and Dave should not get away with what they did. Mom agreed and Dr. Fine called DYFS with us there and reported the info. After she was done answering their questions, she was quiet while listening to the response from the worker on the other end of the line. Then all she said was "I see. Thank you," and hung up the phone. She looked at us and said, "They took the information, but because this happened in New York, they have no jurisdiction. They said the next step would be that they'd transfer the referral to their counterpart in New York state to investigate. They said we could file a complaint with the Deposit police to press criminal charges." I was like, "Do I really have to go back to Deposit? Will I have to go to court?" I was afraid I'd start hyperventilating again. Dr. Fine said that was totally up to me and my Mom. If we don't press charges, it may end up as a legal matter in court anyway if New York's DYFS counterpart finds evidence of abuse and that a worker there may want to interview me and my Mom. That really freaked me out. Dr. Fine said if that happens that she would do everything she could to support me and help me through it. She also explained that abuse survivors often feel empowered by confronting their abusers, but the decision was up to us to pursue it independently of a child welfare organization. She also said that it could take a while to get processed through the system, unless they make it a priority. At the time, I was just in shock. First I tell what happened and now this. I know she had to report it, but I just want all of this to go away. Mom and I went home and sat on the couch together and cried. She held me and kept telling me how sorry she was, over and over. She said we did not have to report it to the Deposit police if I didn't want to. She said she was sorry for not keeping me safe and that she will do whatever it takes to be a better mom. I had an individual emergency session the next day with Dr. Fine. I had to take the day off from school, but I don't think I was in shape to go to class that day, anyway. I told Dr. Fine how I felt. That I was relieved to talk about it, but that I still felt ashamed and did not want to have to go to court and bring all this up again. She told me that my feelings were normal and that I had nothing to be ashamed of. She told me that Dave, even though he was only a few years older than me, was in a caretaker/counselor role and abused his power by forcing me to have sex with him. She said that Rolling Hills was also responsible because they did not provide adequate supervision or oversight of counselors and were letting kids be in charge of kids with no training or appropriate credentials. She said that the program should be shut down and the owners and administration held responsible. All this time I thought it was my fault and I felt like I caused it to happen. She explained that the program essentially brainwashed me and everyone else, including the parents, by telling us that we were addicts (based on a bogus interview) and that everything that happened to us was our fault and responsibility. She was shocked that this was going on and no one knew or ever blew the whistle on them. I felt relieved that she said this, but then I just felt angry that I had to go through it. So we talked about that. She told me that I had every right to be angry, and that she was sorry, and angry, too. We ended the session with a guided meditation to help me relax, and that did help a bit. Now I just feel a mix of emotions. I feel angry and I'm also nervous about what's going to happen with the investigation. I hate not knowing. But at the same time, I'm glad to know that I am not at fault or a bad person. Dr. Fine said I can call and ask for an emergency session if I'm feeling too overwhelmed, but I think I just want to try to get back to normal. I know I can't pretend nothing happened, but I need some time to get used to all of this. I hope my nightmares stop now. Mom said I could take the week off from school, even though I have tests and stuff, but I want to go back to school just to feel normal again.

October 30th, 1986

I've been seeing Dr. Fine twice a week individually, and we put family sessions on hold so that I could have time to "process" all of this. She is not forcing me to talk about it, but I want to. I feel like all these feelings are just coming out and she listens. I feel like she cares. DYFS got back to her and said that the case was referred to New York, and that it was assigned to a worker there who did an investigation. What they found was that Rolling Hills closed! But not for abuse. For insurance fraud! At least no other kids will have to go to that place. But since they don't have enough information about Dave (I never knew his last name), they can't prosecute and don't know if he is still in New York. They can only prosecute if he is in their "jurisdiction." You know what, I'm glad. I didn't want to see him again anyway. I just want to put this whole horrible thing behind me. What kind of world is this where adults use kids to make money? That makes me really angry. I told Mom that all of these places should be shut down, but I guess some of them are legit. The place Justin and Jessie went to seemed like it helped them. Sort of. Maybe this is just a big scam and rehabs are bullshit. AA seems to help people, but I wonder if that's brainwashing too? I just don't know anymore. It's hard to put my trust in anything anymore. Jessie, Justin and I are going to get together this weekend. Tomorrow's Halloween. I'm too old to trick-or-treat so I'll be manning the door giving out candy. People are talking about having Halloween parties. Even if I was invited I wouldn't go. I'll just hang out with Jessie and Justin. This guy in Guitar Club asked me out but I told him I'm busy. I can't deal with guys right now. Dr. Fine is working on that with me. We've been talking about how I have the right to decide what to do with my body, and that it's up to me to decide how sexually active I want to be, not a boy. I am starting to think that all boys want is sex, they don't care about who it's with as long as she's hot. That makes me mad. Although Justin doesn't seem that way. He seems to really care about Jessie. I guess boys are not all bad. Some make good friends.

November 3rd, 1986

So I did end up hanging out with Justin and Jessie last weekend. I stayed over Jessie's house Saturday night and after Justin left we stayed up and had a really good talk. She told me about her rehab experience, and how while she hated being locked up and in a hospital at first, she learned a lot about herself and met some really cool people. She got put in rehab because she was caught smoking pot on school property with her friends, and got suspended until she had treatment. She doesn't feel that her program brainwashed her, but she said it was hard to get used to being back home when she was done after being away for so long. Her program is a 12-month inpatient program. It follows the 12-Steps and kids work on one step a month until they complete the program. They start to transition to weekends back home in the last three months. She didn't get behind in school because she had a private tutor that came to the hospital after the first month. She also had free time there to work on her art, and she showed me some of her paintings. She does these really abstract paintings that are cool. She says it's her way of expressing her emotions. Jessie's parents are very nice, too. They have a huge house. It has three floors and Jessie has the third floor all to herself; one room she uses for her art studio and the other is her bedroom. She also shared with me that she's not really a Deadhead. She likes them, but doesn't love them the way Justin loves them. She really likes classic rock and listens to a station called K-Rock from NYC. She loves Jimi Hendrix and Eric Clapton, but also likes the mellower artists like Joni Mitchell and Cat Stevens. But she does want to go see the Dead when they come around because she has never been to a Dead show and now she's finally old enough that her parents will let her. She said it took a while to earn their trust back after she came home, but now that they see she has not been using and is attending an AA meeting once a week and doing well in school they've calmed down. She said that at first they were really embar-rassed, because she was suspended and all, but they seem to treat her fine now, I think. Her family seems a lot more normal than mine. She has an older brother who is away at college. He'll be home at Thanksgiving. She wants to invite me to Thanksgiving dinner with her family, but I don't know if I feel right about leaving my Mom alone. She said she'll ask if my Mom can come too. I think she just really wants to talk to her about Woodstock. I invited her and Justin to come over this weekend so she'll probably hit my Mom up then.

November 13th, 1986

I am starting to feel better, calmer and the nightmares have gone away, at least for now. Dr. Fine and I agreed that we can go back to once-a-week individual sessions and once-a-week family sessions. Mom says she notices a difference in me as well; she thinks I'm more relaxed. We had Jessie and Justin over for dinner last Saturday night and Jessie stayed over. It went pretty well, I think. Both Jessie and Justin think it is so cool that Mom got to go to Woodstock, so of course they bombarded her with questions: "What was it like? You got to see the Dead and Hendrix, how awesome, how were they?" And so on. They were kind of disappointed that she didn't remember much, but she told them that was because it was a long time ago and she was tripping for most of it and spent a lot of time in a van with people she had just met, one of whom was presumably my father. It sounded like she just went to party, not for the music. She told us she liked all those bands, everyone did back then, but for her it was more about getting out of town and doing something cool with a bunch of people her age. Then she got kind of moralistic about the whole drug thing and said that she made some poor choices and that the best thing that came out of it was me, but that she was sorry she didn't know who my Dad was. Justin and Jessie just sat there with their mouths open. I guess they don't know any parents like that. Neither do I. Their parents, especially Jessie's, are so straight and responsible. Plus, the way my Mom looks now with her short hair that is perfectly styled with mousse and her boring mom clothes, it's hard to picture her as a hippie. I showed them some of the pictures she had sent me from the commune and they thought those were cool. I don't know, to me it's just all normal. But we talked about other things too, and Mom let us hang out in my room and listen to the stereo and left us alone after dinner, which was good. Then Justin's dad came to pick him up at about 11:30 and Jessie and I stayed up talking. I told her about my Rolling Hills experience, and I mean everything. She started to cry when I told her about Dave and what happened after everyone found out. She said she wishes that they all got arrested, not just that the program got shut down. This was the first time I've told anyone besides Mom and Dr. Fine and I got through it OK. I started to hyperventilate a bit, but then did some breathing exercises that Dr. Fine taught me. Jessie gave me a big hug at the end, told me she loved me and that she is so glad I am OK. Jessie is so easy to talk to. She listens, like Dr. Fine, and gives really good advice. She seems a lot more mature than other kids I know. Even the honor student ones, who are just as big partiers as the jocks and metal heads. It seems like most of the kids I know are so boring. All they want to do is go to football games (and I hate football, to me it's just a bunch of guys jumping on top of each other and getting whistles blown at them) and then go party and drink, and the girls live at the mall. I only go to the mall when I need to go shopping. I think it's pretty boring myself. Anyway, what I really like about Jessie is that she is her own person. She doesn't care what anyone thinks, even Justin. She does what she likes and she hasn't even slept with Justin yet because she doesn't feel like she's ready to have sex. And he respects that. I mean, of course they fool around, (not in front of me), but he's the first guy I've met who actually respects girls and treats them as people, not pieces of meat. I hope I can meet someone like him. I think they are pretty rare. I mean I get hit on all the time at school by guys because I guess they think I am hot, but I just have no interest in guys or sex right now. Maybe someday in the future but not anybody I have met so far. Every once in a while I see Tyler at the record store (I don't go in there anymore) and I just don't make eye contact. I'm going to spend Thanksgiving weekend with Jessie because her parents invited me and my Mom since we don't have any family anymore. Then Mom is going home and will go to meetings and hang out with her 12-Step friends over the weekend and I'll stay at Jessie's. She wants to take me to downtown Chester (well, what there is of it). Chester gets a lot of day tourists because it has a lot of antique stores, restaurants and boutiques and people from the city like to come out to walk around. Jessie said there's a really good used record store there so we're going to check that out and buy some albums. If it was warmer out we'd go to the park and I'd play guitar, but it's too cold this time of year. It will probably be really crowded, too, because people are coming to do Christmas shopping and they also have a big flea market that is just off of Main Street. We're going to check that out as well, because sometimes they have cool stuff that's inexpensive. Jessie is Jewish, so her family doesn't celebrate Christmas, they celebrate Hanukkah. Hanukkah actually falls on the day after Christmas this year, which she said rarely happens. It lasts eight days! She said she gets a present every night, but only one big present the first night and then seven small ones the rest of the time. When she was a little kid they played dreidel for chocolate coins, but she doesn't do that anymore. Her mom also makes potato pancakes which they call latkes, and they are basically fried potatoes but sound like they taste good. Her older brother will be there for Thanksgiving. She showed me a picture of him. He's really cute. He goes to college in Connecticut; it's a pretty good school, Wesleyan I think it's called. Jessie doesn't want to go there because she said it's too small and the town is kind of boring. But she said most of the colleges that have good Art programs and good Liberal Arts programs are like that so she'll probably end up at one in a small town. She's a good student and is taking an SAT prep course now just for the PSATs in March. I guess I should start thinking about preparing for them. She has to go all the way to Morristown for the course since they don't have any around here. I have seen study books in the mall at the bookstore. Maybe I'll just do one of them. I usually test pretty well anyway, so I'm not too worried about it. Jessie is though, because in her family it's expected that you go to a really good college. I think that's cool that her family is so educated. They talk about interesting things at dinner like politics and what's happening in the world, and they like to go to art museums in the city and plays and stuff like that. Jessie's mom works in Morristown but her dad is a surgeon in NYC so he works crazy hours. Jessie's mom used to work in the city but after Jessie went to rehab one of the things that came out of family sessions was that Jessie was on her own too much and needed more parenting and structure, so her Mom wanted to be closer to home, especially when she had to work long hours on a case. I'm talking a lot about her. I guess that's because I really respect her. She knows who she is and what she wants. I want to be like that, too.

December 1st, 1986

Thanksgiving weekend was really fun! We went to Jessie's house for Thanksgiving dinner and there were a lot of people there because her aunts and uncles and cousins were there, as well as me and Mom. Justin was invited but couldn't go because he had to go with his parents to visit family in Massachusetts for the weekend. The other person there was Jessie's brother. His name is Jeff and he is just as cute in person as in his pictures. I didn't really get to talk to him much that day because there were so many people there and her family loves to have loud, political discussions at the table (although most of them are liberal Democrats and agree on everything). They were talking about a bunch of stuff that they read in the New York Times and heard on PBS. There was a lot of talk about the Iran-Contra affair, which involved selling weapons to the wrong people (from what I could gather), and talk about the Democrats taking back the Senate. I had no idea about any of this because Mom and I never talk about the news and we don't read the *NY Times*. Jessie's family, her last name is Goldberg, loves this stuff. Jessie is interested to a point, her brother more so. I felt kind of stupid for not knowing much about current events, but I guess I have had a lot on my mind after the year I've had. Mom found the conversation interesting and shared some interesting ideas. I wish she'd talk more about that stuff with me. I'm learning a lot about her these days and it seems like there are so many layers to her that I am discovering. Anyway, I stayed over for the weekend and Mom left Thanksgiving night as planned. Jessie's parents took me, Jessie and Jeff to the city to see an exhibit at the Met on Friday. I had never been there before. That is one huge museum. I like how there is art from all over the world and there is so much history. Jessie spent some time sketching some of her favorite artists and I walked around the museum with her parents and Jeff while she did that. Then we all met up for lunch at the museum café. Jeff tried to talk to me a bit but I didn't know what to say to him. He's so smart and cute and confident. He writes for his school's newspaper and knows so much about politics and current events, and I had no idea what to say to him so I just nodded and listened. I hope he doesn't think I'm just some dumb girl. It got me thinking about how I need to take school more seriously and pay attention to what's going on in the world. There is so much I don't know. But at school we don't really talk about current stuff, it's all memorization and the only class where we really talk about what people think is English, which is why I like it so much. Dates and events without a real meaning bore the hell out of me. It seems like all the good stuff gets learned in college, so I guess I need to focus more on going to a good school. I'm glad I met Jessie and her family; they are so much more interesting than the people I see every day. So on Saturday night Jeff took me and Jessie to the movies and I ended up sitting in between them so Jeff was right next to me! That made me really nervous. His arm kept bumping mine on the armrest and I was having a hard time paying attention to the movie because I am really attracted to him. I was trying not to think about Dave and Tyler and even Kyle, because he is the first guy I have even been attracted to since Tyler and Kyle (Dave is in a whole other category. I still feel guilty that I let him use me, even though Dr. Fine has told me that what happened is not my fault. I guess I still have to work on that). But Jeff didn't hit on me or anything. He was really nice the whole weekend. Jessie told me he doesn't have a girlfriend right now because he was in a really serious relationship that just broke up. She thinks he's attracted to me but doesn't want to make a move because I'm still in high school and thinks I am too young. If he only knew what I've been through. I have probably experienced more than any of his girlfriends have. But he doesn't need to know that. And Jessie swore she would not tell anyone what I told her and I trust her. He is cute though. And smart. I like that. He left Sunday to go back to school and Jessie and I walked around downtown Chester and went to the flea market. Chester has some cool shops, but it's really for the older crowd who like antiques. They do have a really good homemade ice cream shop and a store that sells turquoise and silver jewelry from the Southwest. I wanted to get Mom's Christmas present there, but everything I thought she would like was too expensive. We went to the record store and I picked up a bunch of albums. I was able to get like 10 records because they were used and cheaper than the new ones at regular record stores. I've been into a mix of music lately. I bought a copy of *Workingman's Dead* and *American Beauty* because those are the Dead albums I like, and I like playing those songs in Guitar Club. I also bought Jimi Hendrix's *Are You Experienced*. And some stuff from Peter Gabriel, Steve Winwood and Eric Clapton (they didn't have the new albums from them so I got some of the older ones). I guess Jessie's classic rock taste is rubbing off on me. I've been trying to listen to K-Rock, but the signal doesn't come in as well in Hackettstown for some reason. All we get is the local oldies AM station and the college station. Then after walking around downtown Chester, we went to the flea market and I bought some clothes and did find a Christmas gift for Mom. There was somebody selling really pretty glass vases so I hope she likes it. Well, time to go, I have Dr. Fine tonight.

December 17th, 1986

So my family session with Dr. Fine last week was pretty interesting. I was going to write about it sooner but I had a bunch of tests to study for and a lot of English homework since we are going on break soon. And another book report to do over break. What's the point of having a break if we have to spend the whole time working? My English teacher, who I will forgive because I like him and he's cool, said he's trying to prepare us for college and that we need to learn how to organize our time. Mom is thinking about signing me up for an SAT prep course starting in January, so then I'll have that too. Oh yeah, so Dr. Fine… In our family session we talked about what each of us want from our relationship and she asked us each to pick an activity we'd like to share with each other during the Christmas break. Mom told me that she was taking the week off to be with me and that nothing was more important than us spending quality time together. So Christmas will be just the two of us. We're decorating the tree this weekend, and then we're going to bake cookies on Christmas Eve and open presents and have Christmas dinner on Christmas Day. I was kind of disappointed that I couldn't invite Jessie over since she doesn't even get to celebrate Christmas, but I get that Mom and I need to spend time together to work on our relationship. I told Mom what I wanted was to do some different things in NYC, like go see the tree, and the windows on Fifth Avenue, and I would like to go back to the Metropolitan Museum. I want to get out of Hacketts-town. She thought that was a good idea and she's going to look for some other things we can do in the city, like maybe go to a show or go to Chinatown for dinner or something. I appreciate that she's trying. I am trying to forgive her, but it's not easy. Just when I think I've let go of my anger it will come up when I least expect it. Dr. Fine says not to worry, that it's normal and I'll eventually work through it. I think what's most confusing with my Mom is that she doesn't know how to relate to me. She keeps wanting to be my friend and not a mom and I'm not sure that's what I want. Sometimes I feel like she just tells me too much and sometimes I feel like she doesn't tell me enough. Like about my family. It really bothers me that I had to find out so many things in a family therapy session. But then she'll go on and on about how she feels about things at work or her friends in AA. She says she wants a relationship with me, but she rarely asks me how I feel about things. Sometimes I just wish she would listen to me. She thinks she does but she doesn't. Somehow everything ends up being all about her. Maybe I should bring that up in family session, but I'm afraid Mom will start crying and feel sorry for herself and then I'll feel guilty for getting her upset. And then I'll get angry and isolate in my room because I won't want to be around her and then I'll feel guilty about that. Why do I always feel so responsible for her emotions? Isn't she the one who's supposed to feel responsible about mine? Things were so much less complicated when Gram was taking care of me. She acted like a mom. The rules were the rules and I knew what to expect. Yeah, I found ways to get around them, but Gram was predictable and really did care about what I did and what I wanted. She didn't really ask how I felt about things, but I knew she cared. Mom is just kind of a flake sometimes. I know she means well, but it's like she has no clue about how to be a mom. I like Jessie's mom. She treats Jessie with respect but doesn't let her do everything she wants. And they discuss things, so if her Mom (and Dad) say no, they explain why. That does not happen in this house. Dr. Fine is trying to get us to work on family rules and a contract and all that stuff, and I hate to admit it but I kind of want that. At least I'll know what's expected of me.

1987

January 5th, 1987

The holidays and Christmas break are over and now I'm back in school. I got my book report and other stuff done that I had to, but I waited until the last minute (this past weekend) because I just felt like I needed a break. Now we have to prepare for mid-terms, which are happening in a couple of weeks. Since I'm a junior I really have to study if I want to have good grades to apply to college. I wonder if they'll ask me about sophomore year? My guidance counselor told me that since my credits transferred the course titles and grades will say Hackettstown High School, even though I had a private instructor. Mom signed me up for the Sherman Schwartz SAT prep program. That's the one Jessie goes to. Now, in addition to individual and family therapy sessions each week, I will have to go to Schwartz classes every week in Morristown, but Mom is all in about it and has no problem with driving me there. It's going to be pretty hard for me to have much of a social life in the next couple of months, between mid-terms and getting ready for the PSATs. Not that my life is all that exciting right now, but still…Mom and I did end up doing a lot of the stuff we planned in the city, we took the train most of the time so she didn't have to drive. The weather wasn't great but I really did enjoy dinner in Chinatown even though it was super crowded. I enjoyed going back to the Met and the Museum of Natural History. I really liked the displays of the animals and the dinosaur exhibit, but my favorite was the Planetarium. I heard they used to do laser rock shows there. I wish I could have seen those. I've been practicing songs from the Dead albums I bought. The Guitar Club is going to be part of the junior talent show, so I'm going to be in that. Jessie says I don't have enough activities on my resume for college. I never really thought about that. Aren't colleges just concerned with your SAT scores and grades? Besides, if you're a good student aren't you supposed to be studying? When am I supposed to have time to join more clubs if I have to go to AA once a week, two therapy sessions and now the Schwartz thing? But she says that the good colleges want to see that you are well rounded. She's in like three clubs in her school; I don't know how she fits it all in. I don't think I should have to have a nervous breakdown to go to college. I have to meet with my guidance counselor soon to pick out next year's schedule and talk about post-high school plans, which for me is college. It all feels kind of overwhelming right now. I'm still trying to figure out what I want to major in and where I even want to go. My favorite subject is English and I love to read and enjoy writing so I think I'll probably major in that. But what do you do with an English degree? Teach? Go to grad school? Work for a publishing company? I guess I should just ask my guidance counselor – that is what he gets paid for, isn't it? And then I have to get Mom to take me to visit schools. I learned the hard way that brochures don't tell the whole story. And do I want to stay in-state or go to an out-of-state school? In the city or country? So many decisions! I can feel myself getting overwhelmed as I'm writing this. I guess I should go do my relaxation exercises and then make a list of what actually needs to get done today, not within the next year. Dr. Fine has been working with me on that. Basically, I am working on strategies to organize and prioritize my goals, especially with regard to school, like when things are due and what to focus on first, because that will prepare me for college. Having a plan does help…if I start thinking about it all at once I hyperventilate. I wish Mom could help me and give some advice from her days in high school, but she says she didn't take school seriously, it was more of a social thing for her and an excuse to get out of the house and away from Gramps and farm chores. She didn't study for the SATs or anything, she just took them once and got about 1,000 so she just applied to state schools. And then didn't even go for more than a semester. She says she never really studied that hard, and that she was lucky because school work came easily to her. But if she had put in more effort, I wonder what she would have become? I do admire her for getting her life back together and going to school at night to get her degree. That could not have been easy. I wonder if she misses her old hippie life at all? It seems to me that something must have happened to wake her up and make her realize that things needed to change. I mean, how do you go from stoned hippie to suddenly getting up and going to work every day and being sober? But she did it and something must have motivated her. I guess I can just ask her. I'll tell her I want one of those mom/daughter dinners where we have a "meaningful talk." She loves that shit and she loves to talk about herself for sure.

It's funny, Jessie really likes my Mom. She thinks my Mom should write a book about her experiences. I guess when you have a regular mom like hers, people like my Mom seem exotic. Yeah, well, she doesn't have to live with her. I think her family is much more interesting. They are so intelligent and well read and know so much about so many things. Every time I hang out there I feel like I'm sitting around a bunch of human encyclopedias. But it's cool though. They don't get all judgmental like my Mom's friends from AA. They actually ask my opinions about things and think that even though I'm just 16 going on 17 my ideas and opinions matter. I like that, even if sometimes I feel put on the spot. Jessie's brother is still home but nothing has happened between me and him. I think he thinks of me as a kid sister like Jessie. He's nice to me though and asks me what I think about things, but I don't get any feeling that he is attracted to me or wants to go out with me. I still get that tingly feeling when I'm near him, though. He's not the type I usually go for, but I feel safe around him. He treats me like a person, not a thing to be used to get his rocks off. Well, seeing as how I have so much work to do I guess I need to go do it. But you know what, I don't feel so anxious and overwhelmed anymore. Maybe writing about it works as well as relaxation exercises. But I do think I will plan out my work and due dates in my planner, so enough for today here.

January 14, 1987

Mom took the day off from work today to take me to DMV to get my learner's permit. Now that I'm turning 17 and a junior I'm in Driver's Ed for this quarter instead of Gym and I need a permit to take the class. But I want my permit anyway. I can't wait to drive! I want to try to schedule my road test for right after my birthday so I can drive as soon as possible. Mom promised that she'd take me out for driving practice on the weekends (since it's dark when she gets home from work). That will make my schedule even busier, but I really want to drive and get my license and I need to pass my test the first time out or I won't be able to drive this summer. I also met with my guidance counselor to talk about next year's schedule and college stuff. He wants me to start research-ing colleges and went over all the requirements for four-year schools. Normally they do that sophomore year, but I was locked up in Rolling Hills, so… Anyway, I am thinking NYU because I love the city and they have pretty much every kind of major you can think of and lots of writing and creative type classes. Plus, I love the Village and think it would be cool to live there. So, my counselor recommended that to be compet-itive I need to take Physics and Calc next year even though I don't really like Science or Math that much. I am making it through Chemistry by the skin of my teeth and getting B's and I really just wanted to take stuff I like senior year but he recommended against that. I will have fulfilled my History requirement; I am taking American History II now and getting A's. So I can choose another elective in addition to my three major subjects and Gym, which is another requirement. I thought about an Art class but I don't have Jessie's talent and decided to pick Journalism because then I get to write for the school newspaper and can count it as a club for my college applications. I also picked a new class they are starting called Student Mentor, which doubles as an extracurricular activity. The teacher is one of the guidance counselors (not mine) and people say she's really nice. It is sort of an intro to Psych and Counseling class and we are assigned to an at-risk student as a mentor. My counselor thought I would be a good match because of what I went through with Rolling Hills and my sobriety and stuff. I don't really want to have to talk about what happened there, but he told me that I don't have to talk about myself, I am there to listen to the other student and be supportive and encourage healthy behavior. However, if a student reports drug use or suicidal behavior I am required to report that to an adult and/or school professional and am not allowed under any circumstances to keep it to myself, even if the student asks me to. I get the whole confidentiality thing since I am in therapy myself. He (my guidance counselor) knows that, and what I think is weird is that he thinks I should be counseling other students when I'm getting counseling myself? How does that work? Doesn't he think I'm an at-risk kid? I guess he must think I'm more mature than I think I am. I'm still not used to adults thinking that highly of me. I thought they only liked the good kids who are cheerleaders and student council members and football players. I guess not.

So this Saturday Mom is going to take both me and Jessie for driving practice at the high school parking lot. Mom and Jessie's mom are taking turns with this each weekend since she's in Driver's Ed too. Justin's younger than us; his birthday is in July so he has to take Driver's Ed first quarter next year. He is all excited about the Dead recording their new album and getting tickets for their live show this summer. They're coming to Giants Stadium on July 12 and he is going to get the three of us tickets. I'm glad the show is after school is over so I can relax and enjoy it. Justin and I are doing two songs together as a duet for the talent show in May. We chose one from *Workingman's Dead* and one from *American Beauty*; they are "Candyman" and "Dire Wolf." He wanted to do

"Uncle John's Band" but our teacher said no because the lyrics have "God damn." "Casey Jones" was out because it mentions drugs (cocaine) and "High Time" was out because it could imply doing drugs. Justin really wanted to do "Scarlet Begonias" or "China Cat Sunflower," but we don't have the sheet music for those and I think the harmonies are better on the songs we picked anyway. Plus, only Deadheads know those songs and as it is most people don't know the ones we picked. Anyway, he and I are practicing once a week at Guitar Club and the other kids think we sound pretty good already. I've gotten several compliments about my voice.

So my family session is tomorrow night and I think I am going to bring up my desire to have a heart-to-heart talk with my Mom about why she really got sober. I mean instead of her moral inventory reasons. I am curious about how she became who she is. She's been getting less selfish lately. She is trying to be interested in things that are important to me (like driving!!) and my friends; she loves Jessie and thinks she is a good influence. And she listens when I practice my songs for the talent show. Sometimes I practice with Justin at our house because we need to get the harmonies right and Jessie and Mom are the audience. We'll be doing that this weekend after Jessie and I practice driving. Then Jessie and Justin are going to the movies; they invited me but I hate being the third wheel all the time and so I'm going to see if I can do the mother/daughter thing with Mom Saturday night. Jessie's going to stay over and then on Sunday Mom goes to her meeting and I need to stay home and study and do my homework.

February 3rd, 1987

I have not had time to write because between studying for mid-terms, starting the Schwartz thing, therapy, driving practice and talent show practice I barely have time to sleep, let alone write. I don't know how Jessie does it. She is so laid back. She never seems stressed out or anything. When she needs to unwind she just goes in her bedroom studio and paints with her music on. I sometimes forget she even used to smoke pot. I could see with Justin because he is such a Deadhead, even though he's smart and good at science. But Jessie just seems so relaxed and laid back no matter how busy she is. And now she's started yoga at a studio that opened up in Chester. When does she have the time to do that? She confided in me that she wants to stop going to AA because she's too busy, but as part of her after care she has to attend until she has a year of sobriety post-rehab. That time is coming up and then I'll have to just go with Justin. His parents are making him go, but I can tell he thinks the whole thing is stupid and I bet he is going to smoke again as soon as he can. I may talk to Dr. Fine about leaving AA and see if that is OK because of our contract. I've been sober for over a year, including my time at Rolling Hills, and I don't even want to smoke. It's funny, she said that would happen and it's true. I don't think smoking pot is bad, I just don't feel like doing it anymore. Jessie feels the same way. She says it was just a phase she went through and she's been there, done that. Time to move on. So I had my heart-to-heart with Mom and she had a hard time explaining why she was the way she was. I didn't really find out much more than I know now, but she said she's really glad that we're closer now and communicate better. She and I came up with a contract and house rules that apply to both of us, but mostly me, because she is the adult. Basically, her rule is to leave me alone when I do my relaxation exercises and to listen to me when I talk, and respect my privacy when I need to write in my journal. My rules are to stay sober, follow my curfew for weeknights and weekends (10 for weeknights, midnight for weekends), be honest about where I'm going and she needs to know who I am going with, and if I'm going to be late or she needs to get in touch with me I need to call and/or leave a number where I can be reached. I am expected to set the table for dinner and help get dinner ready, keep my room neat and clean and take out the garbage. I think that's fair. She does most of the cleaning and laundry and gives me plenty of time to study. Dr. Fine is really happy with how our relationship is progressing and feels we can reduce family sessions to once a month unless there's an emergency or we stop communicating. I'm good with that. I could use an extra free night. Maybe I'll try yoga with Jessie once I get my license and can drive. I really hate being dependent on Mom or somebody else's parent to get around. Well, I need to go and do my extra Schwartz homework, which is mostly practice SAT tests and studying vocabulary words. Boring, but I guess it's what I have to do. At least I'll be able to define loquacious.

March 22nd, 1987

PSATs were yesterday. It felt like they took all freakin' day. I think I did OK. I have to admit the Schwartz class did help prepare me so I was pretty familiar with the types of questions and math problems. But we don't get our results for a while. They mail them to us, and then if we qualify for a National Merit Scholarship they send a letter about that, too. I think you need a pretty high score to get that. Like a 1300 or something. I don't remember. Anyway, I take the SATs again in October and those really count, so for the most part these don't matter unless I want a scholarship. Mom told me she has the money put aside for me to go to NYU if that's where I want to go. Of course, I could always go to a state school or County College of Morris and transfer, but that's not what I want. If I was going to do that I wouldn't have agreed to take Physics and Calc next year! It's hard to believe that in a few months junior year will be over and I'll be a senior! I feel like so much has happened to me in the past five years. It's like I've lived a thousand lifetimes. I wonder if other kids feel the way I do? The ones I know at school all seem so happy and they don't care about anything except who is going out with whom and whether the Tigers won and all that. I really don't give a shit about school sports. I think they are so dumb. And people spend so much time on them. There are people who go to every Friday football game, and then every basketball game during the winter and then there is baseball and soccer and the list goes on and on. Hackettstown is so full of jocks. And even the teachers!! Half of them go to all the games! Don't they have lives and kids of their own? And all the stupid spirit activities. Thank God for Justin and Jessie. I would be miserable if I didn't have them. Justin feels the same way but he's kind of a loner, so as long as he has the Dead, his fish tank and Jessie he is good. Well, I think he wants to be able to smoke pot again, but that's another story. If he does I think Jessie will be pissed. But maybe not, she doesn't judge people, but still I mean after spending all that time in rehab, would he really want to get sent back? I would do anything not to have to do that all over again! And I really don't feel like smoking anyway. I'm not even around it anymore. And I don't drink so that kind of limits who I can hang out with, because the jocks and popular kids are always drinking at parties. And the adults look the other way because it isn't drugs. I think that is so hypocritical. I mean, here are all these parents who freak out when their kid smokes a hit off a joint but look the other way when they drink beer at a party. Some of these parents even let their kids drink beer at football parties because at least the kids are doing it supervised in their own home. Really? I think that's bullshit. But I guess I have to get used to the whole drinking thing because everyone says in college it rules your social life. That just seems lame to me. Which is another reason why I want to go to NYU because there is so much to do in the city. I don't have to spend my time getting drunk at frat parties and watching guys tip cows. I can't believe people actually do that. It happens here, too. Well, not in Hackettstown itself, the only cows are in the auction house, except when they escape and run down Main street and the cops have to shut it down. Yes, that happened. Hackettstown is an exciting place indeed. So yeah, cow tipping, that used to happen in Warwick and drive Gramps crazy because it really can hurt the cows. So he always made sure they were in the barn at night. Most of the farms are in the surrounding towns so I guess that's where it happens around here. After all you, can't go cow tipping without cows hanging around. Why am I going off about cows?

Anyway, I am more and more sure that NYU is my first choice. Mom said we could do a visit this summer and that we could schedule an information interview at admissions. I think this summer is going to be pretty busy because I need to get a job as well. Jessie is going to be a CIT at the day camp she used to go to called Washington Lake. It's this exclusive camp that rich kids from closer in to the city go to. Jessie says that it is pretty typical for Jewish kids to go to camp in the summer. A lot of them go to sleep-away camp but some go to day camp. She thinks she can get me a job there so I think I'll do that. I like kids and I like the idea of working with Jessie. At least I'll get a break from all of this school work. Speaking of which I have to finish a Chemistry lab and study for a test.

April 17th, 1987

Finally it's Friday!! I can't wait for school to be over. I feel like I've had more work than I have ever had in my life, and that is without Schwartz school. I passed driver's ed and my written test!! Now I just have to take my road test next month. We had to schedule it after my birthday because I have to be 17, so we were able to get an appointment on Thursday the 21st, before Memorial Day. They don't tell you right away if you pass. That's another thing I have to wait for in the mail. Sometimes my life feels like one big wait. I'm still waiting for my PSAT scores. They should be coming soon. Mom offered to have a barbecue for me and Justin and Jessie on my birthday, which falls on a Sunday this year. I hope it doesn't rain. Jessie wants to come over early and make me a birthday cake. I think that is so sweet! I'll be 17 on the 17th. Weird! Oh, and Justin got the Grateful Dead tickets. They sold out pretty quickly so he said we were lucky to get them. He didn't get taper seats (I guess those are hard to get), but at least we have a pretty good view of the stage. Personally, I didn't want taper seats anyway. Who wants to be sitting in a sea of microphones where someone is telling you to shut up every five minutes because they don't want crowd noise? What, do they think a concert is a library? Of course people are going to make noise. Duh. I'm a bit worried about what it will be like to be around a bunch of people smoking pot and doing acid. Yeah, they do acid. It's like a Grateful Dead cult thing that people trip, like it's still 1969 or something. I've never been around someone on acid. I wonder what they're like? Justin has tripped. He says it's cool because you see trails and colors and things that aren't really there. I can't believe he really did acid; I mean, he was pretty young when he went to rehab so it's hard to believe that he even was allowed to go to a Dead show let alone do acid, but that's what he says. I asked Jessie what she thinks and she kind of agrees, but she doesn't want to call Justin a liar. I think she's losing interest in him. She told me she kind of likes this guy at school who's a senior, but she doesn't want to hurt Justin and is afraid to break up with him. My prediction is that if he slips and/or relapses they are done. He's still going to the AA meeting but Jessie is not. She goes to yoga that night instead. I still want to do that, but Mom wants me to at least get through the summer sober before I quit AA. I can't drive there anyway at this point and I want to be able to get the car when I can drive, so I'm trying to go along with what she says. The meetings aren't horrible; I'm just getting bored with them because no matter what the topic is the discussion is always the same. I realize that we're supposed to support each other in our sobriety, but half the kids my age are only there because they have to be and I don't think they take it seriously. I guess I'll put up with it for another few months.

Mom scheduled my information interview for the end of July, but because it's information-only it has to be a weekday and we'll both take off from work. I'm allowed to miss one day at work. I did get the CIT job at Washington Lake. That's going to keep me pretty busy. I have to be there from 8 a.m. to welcome the kids off the bus and stay until every kid gets back on the bus at 3 p.m., and later if we have a staff meeting. So it's going to be a busy summer. Justin and I have been practicing for the talent show, which is scheduled for May 22nd. They always schedule assemblies and shows and pep rallies on the Friday before a holiday because they know nobody wants to do any work.

April 30th, 1987

I didn't make the cut off for the National Merit Scholarship program and neither did Justin. The principal named all the winners today during announcements in homeroom. When I got home from school I called Jessie to find out if she did, and sure enough... She is so smart!! But I did OK on the PSATs – I got 1150. So I'm going to try to get my score up to 1200 for when I take the real test. But this time I'm just going to do practice tests from a workbook. I don't think I can take another round of Schwartz school. Mom has been good about taking me out for driving practice, she's impressed with my K-turns and parallel parking. I feel pretty prepared for the test; I just hope we don't get rain and my tester isn't mean. I heard some of them can be pretty grouchy. Why take that job if you don't like kids? I wonder if the testers are in a bad mood because they'd rather just sit behind a desk and give eye exams or something. I don't know, but it seems like everybody that works at the DMV is in a bad mood and the lines are so freakin' long. Nobody I know likes to go there. So I'm in the home stretch for my junior year and so far my grades are good. A's in everything except Algebra II and Chemistry, but I'm getting B's in them. So I'm hoping that as long as I keep my grade point average up and do well on the SATs in October I should be able to get into NYU. Jessie is looking at Wesleyan and Oberlin and some of the other small competitive colleges that have good arts programs. She wants to go to a small school. She doesn't want to apply to any Ivy League schools but her counselor told her to apply to at least one. But what if she doesn't want to go and she gets in? How do you turn down an Ivy League school, especially with a Merit Scholarship? But Jessie does what Jessie wants. Her parents said they would support her decision as long as she chooses a good school. Justin is thinking of just going to County. I was like, really?? I mean he's a pretty good student, but his PSATs were low and he refuses to study or go to a prep class. I think he's smoking again. I swear there was one day I smelled pot on him, but never when Jessie is around or we're in school. I don't think his parents drug test anymore, but who knows? We're all getting together this weekend. It's Mom's turn to take me and Jessie driving – her test is two days before mine. She turned 17 last weekend. Her parents took us all out to dinner at this really fancy restaurant in Mendham and let us order whatever we wanted! It must be nice having rich parents. Jessie doesn't seem to care one way or another. I mean, she's not spoiled or anything, but she just doesn't care about material things except for her art supplies. I talk about her a lot. Dr. Fine noticed that. I guess it is because I've never met any kids like her and I really admire her. She is so smart, and talented and focused. Most of the girls I know just care about their boyfriends, hair and what party they get invited to. They are so boring. Jessie's just different. She doesn't really care about what other kids are doing, and she is so comfortable around guys. Guys like her even though she has her own style. I think it's her confidence. She is so comfortable with herself. That's what I admire. She is comfortable in her own skin. I am getting there but I can't imagine ever being as confident as her. She truly does not care what other people think, except for Justin, but even with him I can see her getting bored and moving on.

June 1st, 1987

I passed my driver's test and my temporary license came in the mail today!! I am so excited!!! I can't wait to take the car out. Mom said I can use it this week to go to my AA meeting, to drive to therapy, and I even offered to do the food shopping on Saturday so I can have it to go visit Jessie. I wish I could afford to buy my own car, though I guess I should be grateful for what I have. At least I'll make some money this summer, but obviously not enough to buy a car. If I go to NYU I won't need a car anyway. But living in Hackettstown, life without a car is impossible.

So the talent show went well. People really liked the songs Justin and I performed and we got a lot of compliments. Even from the principal. One more thing I can put on my college application. Finals are in two weeks and then the last day of school is the 19th, which is also graduation night. I'm not really friends with any seniors so I'm not going, and since I'm not dating any seniors I'm not going to the prom either. But all that seems so juvenile to me anyway. As Jessie would say: been there, done that. Mom said that if I stay sober all summer I don't have to go to AA in the fall when school starts. Plus, I can only use the car if I stay sober and I can't risk losing that! She still drug tests me, which I find annoying – I mean, doesn't she trust me by now? But that is one of her rules until I turn 18. Maybe if I continue to test clean after I stop going to AA she'll stop. I hope so. I find the whole thing humiliating. I brought it up at the last family session and that's where we made the agreement about stopping AA. I was hoping Dr. Fine would support me, but since staying sober is part of my contract with her I guess it is what it is. I think she trusts me but she's trying to respect Mom's role as a parent. I will be glad when I turn 18 and I'm my own guardian. I think I am able to judge for myself at this point what is best for me. I know I made some stupid choices before, but isn't that what kids do? Well, I don't want to get the car taken away so I'll suck it up.

CIT orientation starts the Monday after school is over and then camp starts June 29th and goes until August 21st. They have to wait until all the kids are done with school, and the school year ends later in the towns closer to the City. And then they have to make sure that the counselors who are in college are able to finish before they have to be back in school. We have to wear uniforms that are similar to the kids' (t-shirts and shorts) with the camp name and "Staff" on the back. We get paid minimum wage on an hourly basis, but if we do our job well we can get tips from parents. Honestly, having been to camp myself I think it comes down to glorified babysitting, but at least I get to be with other people my age and I'll get to meet some people from other towns and I don't have to stand in a hot concession stand selling hot dogs all day. They have some social get-togethers for the counselors after hours as well so maybe those will be fun. I'm trying to keep an open mind. But no matter what, it will be better than the summer I had last year. Mom and I are going to the shore again for 4th of July weekend and then when I get back I have that Dead show the next Sunday. I'll be dragging at work the next day for sure, but I'm curious to see if they are really as good live as people say. If anything, watching the people will be entertaining. Jessie's brother is back home and he's going to be working at a law firm this summer. Jessie's mom got him an internship because he's thinking of going to law school. I still think he's cute but he's got a new girlfriend and even though she lives in NYC they spend every weekend together. He's still the only guy I have thought about dating. Who else would I date anyway? Nobody at my high school and none of the AA guys. Most of them have girlfriends and I'm not attracted to the single ones. Still, I feel more comfortable being around guys now than I did. It's only been a little over a year since I got out of Rolling Hills but I think therapy has helped because I really do feel much better. I don't have nightmares anymore and I don't need the relaxation exercises as much. I get stressed out about school sometimes, but Dr. Fine says that's normal. It's funny because my goal when I started therapy was to be a normal kid. I still don't know exactly what that means, but I think my life is much more normal than it was. I go to school, I have friends, I get along with my Mom for the most part. I'm planning to go to college. None of those things were true a year ago. AA is always telling us to be grateful. I am grateful about my life being more normal, that's for sure. Even though I'm doing much better I still want to keep my weekly sessions with Dr. Fine. I really think she's helped. I don't have my final schedule for next year, but since I'm going to be a senior I have priority on electives so I should get the ones I chose. Justin didn't make honors English for next year because he let his grades slip and he doesn't qualify. So I don't think I'll be in any classes with him, and even though he's good in Science, he's not taking Physics and not taking Calc. He only liked Bio and he doesn't need any of those classes if he's just going to County. He wants to have fun his senior year. I see the writing on the wall. Jessie is going to dump him. I don't know when but it is going to happen.

June 20th, 1987

School's out!! I did really well this last marking period. All that studying paid off because I made straight A's, even in Chemistry and Algebra II! The finals were not as bad as I thought they would be. Now I can relax for a bit before I start work next week. Jessie has a pool at her house and they just opened it so she invited me over this weekend to hang. Time to work on my tan before Mom and I go to the shore for Fourth of July weekend! Jesse invited Justin over too, but he doesn't have a job yet for the summer and his parents told him he's grounded until he finds one! I know he doesn't want to miss the Dead show so that lit a fire under his ass for sure! I don't know who's hiring now, but usually the Shoprite has something available, so maybe he'll work for them. Jessie told me that guy she liked at school has been calling her. She didn't give him her number so he must have looked it up or something. She's been telling him she has a boyfriend, but she also told me that she is really tempted by him. I think she's bored with Justin. I really do. And I don't think he has a clue. At all.

June 22nd, 1987

We had our first day of CIT orientation today. The camp seems like a good place to work for the summer. We spent the day getting introduced to the people we're grouped to work with. Each counselor has two CITs so there's always an assistant to supervise the kids in case someone gets sick or something. We're allowed two days off, but that's it. I'm going to use mine for the day after the Dead show and my NYU interview. Jessie and I didn't get the same group. I have the five-year-olds and she has the six-year-olds. There are 12 kids in my group. My counselor seems nice. She's a college student at Montclair State majoring in education. Her name is Karen and she lives in Byram, which is where the camp is located. The other CIT seems OK but is really quiet so I didn't get a good feel for her personality. She lives in Maplewood, NJ which is east of here and has a pretty long bus ride in the morning. Her name is Cheryl and she's going to be a senior like me next fall, but is still 16 because she went to private kindergarten and got to start school early. It's a bummer for her because she has to wait to take Driver's Ed until the fall and by then she'll already be 17. So they had us go around to all the different activity sites so that we were familiar with what the kids will be doing and gave us basic instruction about how to supervise them. We don't have to have CPR or lifesaving certification because there are lifeguards at the lake, but we all have to stand around on the dock with these big bamboo poles in case one of the kids looks like they are about to drown. They said not to worry, that is unlikely to happen and that kids have to pass a deep-water test to swim in water that is over three feet anyway. Most of the kids in my group are from Essex county. That seems like a long way to go on a bus every day to Washington Lake, but all the counselors have bus duty and they get extra tips for that. The rest of the week we will have "bonding" orientation activities so that we all know each other. We get one break time each day (we eat lunch with the kids) but we stay pretty busy because when I looked at the schedules there are like five different activities every day, except when there are camp-wide activities like Carnival Day and Color War. Color War is basically like field day at school except the whole camp is divided into green vs. white (the camp colors) and the parents are invited for the day, but that doesn't happen until August. I hope the food is better than what we had at Rolling Hills! I remember the camp I went to that summer I was 12 had food that was OK. I think we ate a lot of hamburgers and hot dogs, but this place has a lunch room kind of like at elementary school. The counselors and CITs get a 10 -minute swim before the kids so we can cool off. Swim is every day after nap time, which is after lunch. Swim lessons are in the morning. Why do camps always do that? It's always cold in the morning and nobody wants to get in the water. So this place has every kind of activity you can imagine: miniature golf, a softball diamond, horseback riding, tennis, playground, lake (of course), radio station(!), arts and crafts including pottery wheels, drama, nature instruction, you name it. The parents who send their kids here must have a lot of money. I don't know what the tuition is but it's got to be pretty high.

Jessie and I have the same break time so we get to hang out then. She takes the bus because she's on a bus route, but I am driving Mom's car so I have to get up really early to take Mom to work and then drive to pick her up when I am done at 4, so by the time we get home and get dinner started and eaten it's like 7 p.m. But I don't go to bed until 11 p.m. so it gives me some time to relax. Of course, I have a summer assignment for honors English, but I'm not going to deal with that until August. So, Jessie and I met these two guys who are CITs from the boys groups of five- and six-year-olds. They are pretty cute. One of them already likes Jessie but she's trying to be good. Of course, he's the cutest one. The cute guys all fall in love with Jessie. The shy one seems to like me and he is pretty cute, too. I'm not looking to start a relationship so we'll see what happens. If we just like each other as friends that's fine. I like having some new people to hang out with. Jessie's guy is named Jonathan and he lives in Livingston and has his own Honda Prelude that he drives to and from work every day! He already graduated high school but is only 17, so he couldn't be a full counselor. He's going to Yale in the fall! Wow! I don't know anybody who is Ivy League material. I feel kind of self-conscious when I talk to him but Jessie can talk to anybody, and especially Ivy League people since her family has a bunch of them. My guy (if you can call him that, I mean we basically just met each other) is 17 like me but going to be a senior. His name is Todd. He lives in White Meadow Lake in Rockaway, which is east of here. The only time I have ever been in Rockaway is to go to the movies or the mall. They have a better theater than H'town and I heard the H'town theater is for sale so it's going to be closing soon. I'm glad I can finally drive so I can get to the movies this summer. Well, my hand is getting tired and I have to be up early to drive Mom and go back to orientation tomorrow.

July 5th, 1987

Well, we just got back home from the shore and I am exhausted. Mom let me drive us home and it took like five hours with all the traffic. Driving in traffic is not fun. At all. But the shore was good. Mom and I decided to pretend we were kids and we did all that kid stuff like play Skee-Ball, eat funnel cake, and go on the rides and stuff. It was silly but fun. Of course, I spent some time laying out on the beach and swimming, but Mom had to stay under an umbrella the whole time because she is really fair skinned and burns easily. As usual, there were also a bunch of kids partying under the boardwalk and making bonfires at night and getting wasted. And there I was, a 17–year-old hanging out with my Mom. But whatever. We watched the fireworks from the boardwalk and they were pretty cool. It was nice not to be working and running around after kids all day. Working at the camp is good. I don't love it, but for the most part the people are nice and the day goes by quick. The kids are so funny and cute. Most of them are really nice and do what we say, but there is one girl who drives me crazy. She's a real brat and her mother called me right before we went to the shore and sounded desperate because her sitter canceled and she and her husband had a wedding to go to and she couldn't find a sitter. I'm not surprised, that kid is a nightmare. And she has no friends – I wonder why. I'm glad I had a good excuse because I'm doing my best to get as many tips as I can. It's a challenge sometimes, though.

So Todd and I have gotten past the "hi" stage. He's actually pretty nice and he likes the same music I do and also writes for his school paper. He's not a Deadhead, though, so he's not going to the show. He's more of a U2 fan. I like them; U2 is pretty good. I've been asking him about what it is like to write for the paper since I'll be doing that myself next year. He's another really smart kid who wants to go to the Ivy League but is applying to like 10(!) different schools (that are all really good). Rutgers is his safe school. So anyway, Jonathan is like totally in love with Jessie and she doesn't know what to do. Justin finally got a job, at Shoprite. He works in the bakery. He managed to get the night of the Dead show off. I think he would have quit if he didn't. Then his parents would have grounded him again. But he's going and it's all he talks about. The new album *In the Dark* comes out tomorrow and the radio stations have already been playing it. Justin says they get advance copies. The song I heard was pretty good. The radio has been playing "Touch of Grey" and I like that song. I'll get a copy tomorrow if the record store is still open when I get home. Thank God I can go back in there because Tyler doesn't work there anymore! I never see him around town either; I wonder if he moved? He must be done with County. I don't think he is doing a show for the radio station either. Sometimes I listen to it because nothing else comes in well except for that AM oldies station, and now that I don't have to worry about Rolling Hills and their crazy rules I have no desire to listen to oldies. Mom likes that station, though, so she puts it on when she's home during the day. I think they go off the air at night. That is so lame. But that's H'town. I can't wait until I can live in the city. My NYU interview is this month; I'm kind of nervous about that. I hope they like me. I mean, not that it counts for real. I still have to apply and get accepted but I'm thinking I want to apply for early admission/ decision so I'll have everything decided by December 1. I just want it all decided so I can relax during my senior year. Even if my classes are hard, if I get B's the second half of the year it won't matter so much. Well, I am really tired and it's back to work tomorrow, so time to go.

July 12th, 1987

Ok. So the Dead show was…an experience. It wasn't just the Dead; Bob Dylan played with them. Mom was all excited about that when she heard. She is a big Dylan fan. I had no idea who he was. I ended up driving because Justin doesn't have his license yet and Jessie couldn't get the car since her brother was using it. He was originally going to go to the show with us but Justin could only get three tickets and the show sold out quickly. Anyway, we get to Giants Stadium two hours early and already a gazillion people were there. There were vans and cars and trucks with people barbecuing and blasting boom boxes with Grateful Dead music, and a ton of people selling tie-dyed t-shirts all custom-made, and hippie clothes and jewelry, you name it. Oh, and pot cookies, brownies and acid. So we were hanging out by my car waiting for them to open the doors and this guy in a tie-dyed shirt, made in Jerry's likeness, and ripped jeans and moccasins comes up to us and is like, "Duuuude! I got doses for you." And he whips out what I later learned was blotter acid. It looked like tiny postage stamps to me and I was like, "Is this guy nuts? Why is he selling us stamps?" But I kept my mouth shut because I didn't want to sound stupid. Jessie leaned over and whispered in my ear, "He's selling acid," and she said, "No thanks" and I said the same. But Justin was like, "Oh, awwwesome." Then he bought two and took them. So there I was trying to wrap my head around the fact that one, he just broke his sobriety, and two, he broke it in front of Jessie. She was pissed but didn't say anything, which was weird. I just looked at her like now what? Ten minutes went by and he didn't seem any different. When I used to smoke pot, I would feel it kick in about 10-15 minutes after the first hit. I thought the acid was fake. And then about an hour or so later it kicked in. We were starting to walk up to the stadium to get on line to get in and he starts going off about how the crowd of people was like the sea and how awesome it was. OK, right. Plus, everything was making him laugh and he was talking to himself. Jessie just ignored it. We got up to the line and there were people dressed like it was Woodstock and they were holding signs that said, "Need a ticket" and "Need a miracle." Jessie just told people sorry, we didn't have tickets. She said usually there were scalpers but I guess they got rid of their tickets already. There were more home-baked goods for sale but I didn't take a chance because I wasn't sure what was in them. They finally opened the doors and the mass of people headed inside. Jessie and I had to hold on to Justin to make sure he didn't get swallowed up by the crowd. Somehow we found our seats, which were pretty high up. Justin was going on about how he needed to get down to the floor and somehow we convinced him the show would be good where we were. The Dead finally came on and

I recognized the first three songs because they were from the new album, but then I didn't know what they were playing. Jessie was up and dancing the entire time. She knew all the songs. Justin just sat in his chair going "Wooh, awesome." I was there for the duration so I decided to make myself comfortable and crowd-watch. The audience was almost as entertaining as the show. Girls and guys dancing and spinning around and waving their arms. There was a whole section of tapers which was down by the soundboard; it looked like a press conference on steroids with all those microphones. And then there was the light show going on by the stage. It felt like the show went on for hours and I guess it did because they did three sets (and long ones) and then when I thought the show was over Jessie said not to leave because there would be encores and sure enough there were. Two of them. And Dead songs are not three-minute songs. They go on forever. Personally, I thought they were a bit sloppy, especially on the vocals, and I don't get what people love about Dylan; I think he is a shitty performer and his voice sucks. Everybody seemed to be having a good time except for this one guy near us who passed out and security had to get the ambulance. Justin was in his own world tripping and his pupils were HUGE. I've never been around someone tripping before. I wonder if that was how my Mom was at Woodstock. Justin seemed pretty out of it. Awake and happy but totally gone. When it was time to leave and go back to the car, Jessie said to wait for a bit for the crowd to thin out so that we could keep track of Justin and get him back to the car with us. I have to say I am really proud of myself and Jessie because we didn't even have a hit of pot, so I didn't have to worry about driving home.

Jessie said the cops would be all over Route 3, ready and waiting to give out DWIs and bust people and stuff. Somehow we got Justin and ourselves back to the car; it took a long time because he kept stopping to check things out and comment about them. Jessie was holding it together pretty well considering how pissed off I knew she was. We got Justin in the back seat where he lay down and continued to murmur about nonsense and Jessie sat up front with me. Acid takes a while to wear off so we were worried about what would happen when I dropped him off at home. We let Justin off first because he lives closer to Route 80. All the lights were off and nobody woke up so he made it into the house OK. But the next day was another story. I was glad I took off from work because I slept until noon. And got woken up by Jessie calling to say that she had called Justin's house and was going to break up with him. But she didn't have to because his Mom answered and said that he was in big trouble (I guess they figured out he was on something) and was not available to come to the phone and was on his way back to rehab. For at least a year. And she didn't want either of us calling that house again. So no more Justin. Jessie said she was relieved because now she didn't have to break up with him and was free. I was afraid something like this would happen because I had a feeling Justin was using again. And now he lost Jessie and was back in rehab. I wonder if it is the same one? I hope he's not in a place like Rolling Hills. We had some kids like him. Not many. Most made up all kinds of stuff just to "confess," level up and get out of there, but there were some who actually did drugs like acid. Just no junkies or anything like that. It's so weird how you can spend so much time with someone and poof, they're gone. All because he made a dumb choice. Well, I guess I should go make coffee and some breakfast before it's time for dinner.

July 19th, 1987

Jessie and I went on a double date to the movies with Jonathan and Todd last night. We saw *Blind Date* with Bruce Willis and Kim Basinger and laughed our asses off. That is one funny movie. The end was a bit over the top, but I was glad they ended up together. Jessie seems relieved that Justin is out of her life. I ended up sitting in between Jessie and Todd.

Todd is still pretty shy and I can tell he likes me because he put his arm around the back of my chair, but not around me. I like that, I feel safe with him. He seems OK with just being friends for now. Jonathan kissed Jessie goodnight. I bet he is beyond thrilled that she and Justin broke up.

Next Saturday is my NYU interview. I was surprised Admissions is open on a Saturday, but I guess they do that one or two days in the summer for student visits and stuff. We're going to take a walk around the area (there really isn't a campus). Mom wants me to visit some other schools just in case, but I think my mind is made up, so I only want to visit other schools if I don't get in to NYU. I'm going to apply to state schools anyway just as a back-up. Camp will be over in a few weeks and we are in the middle of Color War. Personally I think it's silly, but I act like I'm all excited because the kids really like it. We have to make up songs and things so I'm working on that. I have not done any of my English summer assignment yet. I guess that's going to end up getting done at the end of August. Oh well, I'll write more after my visit.

July 27th, 1987

Just when I thought my life was getting back to normal it happened. I think I might have met my father – and he's a woman. Well, sort of. He's a man who dresses, speaks and acts like a woman and has a woman's name. Marsha. Marsha Weinstein. There's a name for people like that…oh yeah, transvestite. She/he (what do I call this person? She. I guess, or just Marsha) works as a waitress during the day and plays piano and sings in cabarets at night. Apparently Marsha has also been in some off-Broadway – or is it off-off-Broadway shows – and was an understudy for a Broadway show once as well. I met her when we went out to lunch after my NYU interview. I thought I would be writing about that (it went well by the way). Holy shit, I met a woman (or a man dressed as a woman) who could be my Dad, and not only that, he's a gay transvestite! I swear to God. And he doesn't even hide it. Who has a father who is not only gay but a transvestite?? I didn't think that was possible. I mean, how would a gay man sleep with my mother? Was he dressed as a woman and then took off his underwear and Surprise!!

I guess I should start from the beginning. Mom and I had just finished my interview and taken a quick tour around the school and we were starving so we went to a café in Greenwich Village. It was one of those health food places, with vegetarian food like hummus and tempeh and burgers made out of beans. Whole-grain bread and spider plants hanging from the ceiling. Our waitress (Marsha) comes over and introduces herself, takes one look at my Mom and says "You look familiar. Didn't we meet at Woodstock?" I was like, "What??" Here was this woman who looked kind of masculine and had a very deep voice for a woman, but with a dress and boobs and she thinks she knows my Mom?? So my Mom says, "I did go to Woodstock, but I don't remember much." And laughs like that is an inside joke. "I thought so," said Marsha, who then says, "but I used to be Mark then." At this point I am like "What the fuck is going on?" She (Marsha) then explains that she remembers picking up a girl on Route 17 on the way to the show who had the same strawberry blond-colored hair and looked just like my Mom. He says, "Paula right?" At this point I am like, "What is this, the fucking Twilight Zone??" And my Mom says, "Yes, my name is Paula and I remember hitching a ride with a car full of people from SUNY New Paltz. But I don't remember much after that. It's all an acid haze." "Oh," says Marsha, "we had a very good time. Especially me, you and Doug. Of course, that was before I came out so it was the first time I made it with a man in a threesome. That acid was out of sight. Doug is now my partner, you know. He's a successful off-Broadway producer and I play and sing at Eighty-Eights. I was an understudy once for *Godspell* and I was an extra in the movie version of *Hair*, but mostly I just perform in cabarets and some off-off-Broadway shows. Paula…I can't believe I am seeing you in the flesh! Is this your daughter? She is bea-u-ti-ful! What's your name, sweetie?" That was directed at me. I just stammered my name. "Uh, Devon?" I said. Then I noticed them. His eyes. They were exactly like mine. The same exact color. And his nose and jawline. Mine. That's when it hit me that this woman might be my father. Mom noticed it too. It got real quiet and she looked from me to him and got teary-eyed. Then she spoke. She said, "I think you might be Devon's father." I just sat there stunned. After all these years, I could be looking into the eyes of my father. "Really?!" Marsha asked. "This bea-u-ti-ful creature could be my daughter??" Then she/he started to cry. "I am overcome." Marsha said, "If this is true it's just wonderful!!" I just sat there speechless. "Well" said Marsha, "we need to find out. I'll just have to get a paternity test." Mom, able to speak before me, said, "Devon is that what you want?" I just sat there with my mouth open. Could this be really happening? I thought about all the years that I just wanted to know who my father was, and here we are in a restaurant in Greenwich Village being waited on by a transvestite who looks like me and thinks he's my father. I just wanted my life to go back to normal, (whatever that is) so I said, "Can we order lunch now?" "You know what, honey, I'll just take my break early and get someone to cover for me. I'm going to have lunch with my daughter!" And then she/he walked off. I looked at my Mom. "Do you really think he could be my Dad?" I asked. "I mean, yeah, he looks like me – oh, I mean she, what do you call a transvestite anyway?" My Mom looked at me and said, "I don't know." "What don't you know?" I asked. "If he/she could be my Dad or what you call someone who's a transvestite?" She looked at me and said, "Marsha, I guess. Do you want to get tested and find out? I know you're not 18 yet but with both Marsha's and my permission we can get it done. It's a pretty simple test." "I don't know…I guess…this is still a shock, " I said. Then Marsha came back and another waiter came over and took our order.   I was so shocked I wasn't hungry anymore, so I just ordered some "healthy" soda and a salad. And Marsha and Mom just started talking about their lives since Woodstock. When Marsha asked about me I didn't know what to say. How could I explain what my life has been like? I just told her that I had interviewed at NYU and wanted to go there. What else could I say? That I was trying to live a normal life after getting out of a crazy cult rehab? I just let them talk. Then, on the way home, I asked my mother why she never tried to find out who my Dad was. I mean, here he (she) is living in NYC and obviously wanted to know about me and she just never took the time to find out?? I was freaking so I asked her that. She started to cry, and said she was too embarrassed to try to find my father, especially because she knew she slept with more than one guy. She said that she just wanted to pretend the father didn't exist, it was a mistake, she was on drugs, blah, blah, blah. And I have to meet my father, a transvestite, in a restaurant by accident?? Well, if he/she really is my father, I mean we don't know yet. Dr. Fine will love this. We must be the craziest family she has ever had to work with. Do I want to know if Marsha is my father? Well, yes and no. I just want to be normal and I don't think my life ever will be. I haven't even told Jessie yet. She'll probably think it's cool, but I need to talk to Dr. Fine first. I'm still trying to wrap my head around this. I mean, I go into the city for a college information interview and tour, and wind up meeting a person who may be my father?? I was able to get through work today and the kids and busy schedule took my mind off things. I have an appointment to talk to Dr. Fine tomorrow night and then a family session Thursday night. I'm skipping my AA meeting this week. Mom said it's OK since I have two therapy sessions and have been clean on my drug tests. I'm exhausted but wired. I guess I'll do my relaxation exercise and try to sleep. Tomorrow will be a busy day.

July 28th, 1987

I had my session with Dr. Fine tonight. I told her all about Marsha and how confused I was and how I had wanted to know for so long who my Dad was and now this. She helped me sort out how I was feeling and assured me that all of my feelings were normal. Just that by itself helped. She also assured me that I'm not crazy, my family isn't crazy, that the '60s were a time period of dramatic social and political change and had a big influence on people. She also explained that many families have a history of incest and alcoholism, but that people just don't talk about it in public, so it seems more unusual than it is. She also explained that in the case of Marsha, some people are just born in the wrong body and are not happy until they can really express who they are. I never thought about that. I mean, I'm a girl and have always felt like a girl. I can't imagine what it must be like to be one sex and feel like another. At least I don't have that to deal with. Dr. Fine also explained that homosexuality is more common than people think, but there are people who are against it because of either their religion or a lack of understanding. She added that often people who are gay try to have hetero-sexual relationships when they're young because they want to feel "normal" and don't understand about their sexual preferences. Hippies were more tolerant of different sexual lifestyles in general and were rebelling against their parents so people started to come out of the closet more and exper-iment with different aspects of sexuality. My health teacher never explained any of this. All we ever talked about was birth control methods, abstinence and the diseases you can get including AIDS. In fact, one day, I swear to God, the teacher was talking about condoms and said that they fit all sizes and whipped out a banana and a cucumber and demonstrated how to put on a condom. The class was laughing so hard that the vice principal came down to see what was going on. Homosexuality was never mentioned. It's like it didn't exist.

And nobody at school would ever admit to being gay. Being called "gay" is like the worst insult you can give somebody. It makes me wonder if there are gay people walking around my high school who are hiding who they are. Marsha seems so comfortable with herself. It's like she's proud of who she is and doesn't care who knows it. I guess people are like that in the Village. It's one of the things I like about it. You can be yourself and nobody gives a shit. I'm going to talk about this again in the family session and I think I do want the test. I want to know for sure if Marsha is my father or not. Even if she is a woman (sort of). She seems like a really nice, funny and intelligent person and if she is my Dad I'm OK with that. I just won't tell anyone at school. I don't think they'd get it. At all. Jessie will though. I feel like I can tell her anything. She is so open-minded.

August 15th, 1987

Marsha got tested and she IS my father. I feel relieved that I finally know. She wants me to come spend a weekend with her and her partner, Doug. Doug apparently is still a man, even though he's gay. Mom is fine with that if I am. I'm thinking about it, but I probably will. I mean, I have a father now! Even if he is a woman. She seems like a nice person but I am a bit nervous spending a whole weekend with her and Doug. I mean, I don't even know them!!

Camp is winding down and we're finally done with Color War. Green won. I'm actually going to miss some of the kids; I enjoyed being with them. I'm going to Jessie's later and we're going to hang out by her pool. We have another double date tonight with Jonathan and Todd. Jessie is officially going out with Jonathan. I still only like Todd as a friend and I know he wants more, but I told him I just want to be friends and he's taking it pretty well. Besides, school is going to start soon and we won't be around each other every day. I'm going to be really busy with my college application and my classes so I won't have much time to see him. I'll go out on double dates but that's about it. I think Jessie wants to be alone with Jonathan anyway. Dr. Fine, Mom and I agreed that I can stop going to AA meetings. I'm glad. It's one less thing to worry about fitting in. I'm looking forward to my Journalism class. Todd's been giving me ideas about articles I can write for the paper. I think I'm going to do a feature on a different teacher each month. I'll interview the teacher about his or her likes and dislikes and interests so that readers can get to know them as people. Most kids think teachers just sleep in the closet at night. I'm going to Barnes & Noble to buy an SAT workbook and I can use that to prepare for the test in October. Now I have to get going on my summer English assignment since school starts in a couple of weeks and I need to get to the mall for back-to-school shopping. It feels like this summer has just flown by!

September 5th, 1987

So I'm back in school and a senior! It's hard to believe that I'll be graduating in a few months and starting a totally new life! I met with my guidance counselor and we talked about college applications. I told him that NYU was my first choice and he thinks I am a good candidate for early admission. My application and recommendations are due by October 1st, which is before SATs, but I can have the testing service send my results directly to NYU so they have them in time for decision day, which is December 1st. I hope I get to see them before they do. What if I don't score high enough? My guidance counselor explained that even if I don't get early admission I can still apply for regular admission. He wants me to consider at least 10 schools. That is a lot of applications! But I can use the same admission essay for all of them. I've been thinking about what to write. NYU's application asks me to write about an experience that changed my life. Which one? Should I write about rehab or learning who my father was, or even the day I moved in with my Mom? I'm going to talk about it with Dr. Fine when I see her next week. I have to get started on it soon. And I already have a lot of work for my classes. Who are the people who get to coast during senior year? Not me. Uh oh, I'm starting to feel overwhelmed. Time to do some relaxation exercises. Then I promised Mom I would stay in tonight and watch a video with her so we have some mother/daughter time. Jessie's on a date anyway. Tomorrow I'll be doing a mountain of homework and probably a practice test. My favorite class so far is Journalism. I really like the teacher and he likes me. I'm going to ask him to write one of my recommendations. I am also going to ask my honors English teacher, since he has known me for a long time. Then I just need one from my guidance counselor. Ugh. So much to worry about. Time to make a list and schedule. But first I am going to relax. Oh, and tell Mom not to interrupt me for 30 minutes.

September 13th, 1987

I just got back from spending the weekend with Marsha and Doug. I really like them. They live in a really gorgeous townhouse near Christopher Street with their dog Pepe. Pepe is a toy poodle. I like him, too. He's very friendly and doesn't jump all over me the minute he sees me. He is very calm and just likes to be petted. But he does have an annoying yappy bark. The townhouse is immaculate and they have all this very modern furniture. It's three floors but they rent out the top floor to a lesbian couple. I met them and they seem OK. They didn't really spend much time with us when we were there. So, Doug and Marsha love plants. They have a ficus in their living room and hanging plants in the kitchen. The dining room has this really unusual light fixture that looks like it belongs in a museum. There was not a speck of dirt anywhere. How do they keep it so clean with a dog? I stayed in the guest room which was across the hall from their bedroom. They have their own bathroom in their bedroom so I had the hall bathroom to myself, which was good because at least I had some privacy. The guest room, like the rest of the house was really nice, not much furniture, just a double bed and dresser and nightstand, and of course plants. One on a stand and one by the window.

Anyway, we all had fun. Friday night we went to see Marsha perform at Eighty Eights. She has a great voice! Doug calls it sultry. I looked that one up; it's a good SAT word. I knew a lot of the songs she performed because most of them were from Broadway shows, and then someone requested Ethel Merman. I was like, "Really?" Personally, I think Ethel Merman's voice is super annoying but the crowd went wild over "No Business Like Show Business." They were all singing along, including Doug, but not me. I hate that song. It's too overdone. Afterwards we went for a cup of tea (well I did, Doug and Marsha had a nightcap). We were in this café on 4th Street and they seemed to know everybody there. People kept stopping by our table to say hi and then of course they had to introduce me. I didn't know what to say to them. Nobody seemed shocked that I was their daughter. People kind of took it in stride. And Marsha and Doug loved telling them that I was conceived at Woodstock. People loved that. I didn't; it was kind of embarrassing. Saturday they took me to the Museum of Modern Art because I've been wanting to go there, and Saturday night we went to see an off-off-Broadway production in the Village that a friend of theirs was producing. It was kind of silly. It was a musical poking fun at gay culture and had all these songs making fun of heterosexual people who are "manly." There was one number where a bunch of guys were dressed up as the fruit from Fruit of the Loom underwear and they were making fun of a guy dressed up as a steak. The acting and singing were good though. I asked Marsha and Doug why the show was making fun of gay people. After all, isn't that kind of insulting? But they explained that it was actually poking fun at the ignorance of straight culture. Not sure I get that, but nobody seemed offended and people were laughing in all the right places, so I guess it went over well with the crowd. It is interesting seeing a whole different way of life. In the Village, people just do their thing and express affection in public and nobody bats an eye. I wish the rest of the world was so accepting and tolerant. It isn't where I live. That's why I really hope I get into NYU, if not early admission then regular admission. I'm writing a personal statement as part of my application specifically stating why NYU is my first choice and why I want to go there. Hopefully that will help. I spoke with Dr. Fine about my essay and decided that I will write about my rehab experience (not the sexual part though, I don't feel comfortable sharing that) and how it affected my life and what I've done to overcome my pain. She wants to read it when I'm done. I appreciate that, I really do. Anyway, now I have a bunch of work to do before tomorrow so I better get to it.

October 18th, 1987

SATs were yesterday. I was exhausted by the time I was done. I think I did OK. At least I hope so. I practiced every day for a month and finished my workbook. I felt like all I did was SAT prep. In fact, in honors English we were working on that as well. So I concentrated more on the math since in Calc they were just focusing on Calc. Which in and of itself is enough of a challenge. So, my life has been SAT prep, school, homework and my first interview for Journalism class. Our school newspaper is called The Hackettstown Low Down. My teacher loved my idea about interviewing teachers so now my job is to interview one teacher a month. I have to come up with questions, make sure I quote accurately and represent accurately, spell correctly, keep the piece to 400 words (I have to count my words??). Oh, and focus on who, what, where, why, how and when. And get everything done by the third week of the month, which is next week. So my social life is nil. Oh, and I don't know how I could forget this, but in the middle of all this, I had to get my NYU early admission application done and I was stressing about my essay, but Dr. Fine really liked it and so did Mom and Jessie. I haven't had time to hang out with Jessie at all and won't until I get this Journalism interview done. But we have plans for Friday night to hang out and do a girl's night here at my house, and then we're going on a double date with Jonathan and Todd for a Halloween party at Jonathan's house. It falls on a Saturday this year and it's a costume party so now I have to think up some kind of costume. OK, deep breaths. I don't have to do all this today. One of the helpful things AA taught me is to take things a day at a time, or if necessary, a minute at a time. I am really proud of myself for staying sober even without AA. I'm sure someone will have beer or pot at the party (it seems like even the honor students do) but I don't think Jonathan and Todd's friends are the type to be all about getting high or drunk. So I don't think I have to stress about that. Besides, I really don't think most kids care about what I do, they're just worried about themselves. Dr. Fine says that's normal for teenagers. She explained that feeling self-conscious and concerned about peers is perfectly normal at my age and most people are so worried about their own problems and insecurities that they're not even thinking about mine. I feel fortunate that I've finally met some real people who aren't all about looking good and being popular. I told Jessie about my Dad. She thought it was cool and wants to meet him and his partner. I told her that I would ask my Dad if it was OK to bring her with me the next time I visit. Of course, she would have to get permission, but I think her parents are pretty open minded. OK, I have procrastinated enough, time to get some more work done.

November 1st, 1987

I can't believe it's November already! The first marking

period is ending and before I know it Thanksgiving will be here. Marsha, aka my Dad, invited me to visit them for Thanksgiving. In fact, he invited my Mom too, so we're going there and since Mom has to work Friday, she's going to come home and I'll stay with Marsha and Doug for the weekend. I really want Jessie to meet them and they are all for it, and Jessie's parents are cool with it but they want her home for Thanksgiving, especially since her brother is coming home. I still kind of like him but I don't see that going anywhere. I hardly ever see him anyway. The Halloween party was good. Jonathan and Todd's friends were nice, but since they already knew each other they were kind of cliquish and I'm not good at small talk and starting conversations with people I don't know. Dr. Fine said that I'm an introvert and that's fine, it's just a personality type. I've been reading about introverts. Apparently more people are extroverts and fewer people are introverts, so introverts can feel like they're weird. It helps knowing that because now I know there are other people like me who don't want to be the life of the party and are happy with one or two good friends. I'm not sure what to do about Todd. He still really wants to be my boyfriend, and he treats me really well and listens to what I say and is so respectful. But, I just am not attracted to him that way. I really like him as a person and a friend but that's it. Meanwhile, Jessie and Jonathan are still hot and heavy. She told me they've already slept together. After everything I've been through the thought of sex makes me queasy. I mean, I still get attracted to guys (like Jessie's brother), but right now sex just feels…dirty. I'm working on that with Dr. Fine because I know that sex with the right person can be beautiful, but will I ever find that person? It seems like the guys I'm attracted to want to just use me for sex and don't really want a relationship, and the guys who do want a relationship I am not attracted to. Maybe that will change in college. Speaking of college, it is one month from decision day. I'm pretty nervous about that, but my guidance counselor said not to worry and to apply to places other than

NYU as a back-up, so I am. At least I have my essay done. Thank God I don't have to write a separate essay for all of them. I'm applying to Montclair State and Rutgers. Montclair is my safe school, and Rutgers has a really good reputation but I don't want to go there. I kind of don't know why I'm applying there except that my guidance counselor talked me into it. I'm also thinking about Boston University and Temple University. Mom doesn't want me to go too far from home. Jessie thinks I should apply to some of the smaller Liberal Arts colleges, but I don't want a small school either. I really just want to go to NYU. I guess the worst that will happen is if I don't get in anywhere I apply I'll just go to county for two years and transfer, but I don't think that will happen. I'm looking at some Connecticut schools and some in upstate NY like SUNY Albany and Cornell, but I think Cornell is a stretch for me. And I really don't want to spend four years in Ithaca either. At least I don't have to have those applications done until early next year. Well, time to get some work done…

December 7th, 1987

I GOT IN, I GOT IN, I GOT IN!! I am so happy!! Early admission and everything! NYU here I come! Now I can relax (well, sort of) and I got 1300 on my SATs so I don't have to retake them either! What a relief! Plus, I don't have to worry about the other applications now. Mom is sending my deposit in this week and taking me and Jessie out for a celebration dinner. Christmas is coming so we have to start getting ready for that next weekend. I'm hoping to spend some time over Christmas break with Marsha and Doug. They invited me to live with them for the summer before school starts and they can get me a waitressing job near their place. I think I'm going to do it. I'm ready for a change. Jessie is going to Israel for the summer to work on a kibbutz (it's a family tradition). She hasn't applied for early decision anywhere so she won't know where she is going until April 1st. Now she's saying

Oberlin is her first choice. Why would anyone want to go to Ohio for college? That seems kind of boring to me. But she says it's a good school and has a lot of opportunities to create an individualized program. I guess that's good for her. She was thinking about Hampshire College as well, but Oberlin is more competitive. Anyway, now I can just focus on getting my homework and Journalism projects done and relax and have some fun for the rest of the school year. Todd wants to hang out and I guess I will, but only as friends and I have made that clear. He seems disappointed but still wants to hang out with me. He's been really helpful with my Journalism class. He applied to Boston University early admission and got in so he's feeling good about that. Marsha and Doug said it's OK for Jessie to stay over one night with me at their place so we'll do that over the break, and Jonathan and Todd can meet us in the city somewhere as well. I can't believe 1987 is almost over. So much has changed in a year. But in a good way. I'm busier than I have ever been but I feel productive and good and best of all my mood is better. I feel much better about myself and less worried about everything. Finally, everything in my life seems to be coming together.

1988

January 14th, 1988

Well another year has come and gone. Now it's a new year again. I can't believe that in six months I'll be a high school graduate. I kind of wish I could graduate early. Some people in my class are doing that because they have enough credits. But I need to do the full year or risk my admittance to NYU. I'm holding my own with my grades, not straight A's but all B's and above. Honestly though, it feels like a struggle to get through Calc and Physics, but I'm enjoying my Journalism and English class. I can't wait until I can take the classes I want to take when I get to college. I have some required classes, but for the most part I can take what I want. I'm looking forward to living with Marsha and Doug this summer. I had a good time with them over the break and Jessie really likes them, too. I am going to miss her, more than anyone here in Hackettstown. But I think we'll stay in touch. We both have time to hang out a bit more now that college apps are done and we're in the second half of senior year. She broke up with Jonathan because she doesn't want a serious relationship right now and wants to be free for the summer and for when she goes to college. She told me she felt like he was getting too serious and demanding too much of her time. I think she wants to go out with that guy from her school, but she hasn't said that yet. I'm still friends with Todd but I don't really call him that much. He still calls me but I've been saying I'm busy. I like him and all but he lives far away. Now that Jessie is free, I would rather just hang out with her on the weekends. My high school is trying something new this year called Project Graduation. They are trying to prevent drinking on graduation weekend. In order to attend, you have to have no disciplinary referrals, keep your grades above a C, and miss no more than one day of school unless you have a doctor's excuse. Everybody meets right after the graduation ceremony and takes a bus to a surprise destination for the weekend. There are adult chaperones, but they promise that they're picking something cool for us to do. I haven't decided if I want to go. I'm not really close to anyone in my class and I think I would rather just spend my time with Jessie and Mom. Mom and I have been having some really good talks lately. Our relationship is much better now and I actually enjoy hanging out with her. I'm going to miss her this summer and she told me that she's going to miss me as well, but she thinks it is good for me to spend time with Marsha and Doug. Mom and I are going to spend a week at the shore after graduation and then I'm going to move in with them for the summer. Mom said I could invite Jessie to come as well and make it a "girls" week. That sounds fun. Anyway, we've been having these long talks lately. I've been asking her about her life on the commune and why she joined. It's helped me understand her better. Dr. Fine is really happy about our progress and we all agreed to stop having family sessions. I just go individually now and only every other week, because Dr. Fine and I agreed that I'm ready to move on when I graduate. I'll miss her, but I'm feeling much better and have a better sense of who I am and what I want, so it's time to wind things down. Well, I have Physics homework to do and a test tomorrow so I need to go study.

February 16th, 1988

Wow it's been over a month since I've written in here… It's funny I just haven't felt the need. Not because things are bad or anything. Actually, life is pretty good. I'm doing well in school, I've interviewed five teachers so far and everyone likes my articles in the school paper! People are starting to talk to me more and I've been having lunch with some of the kids from my Journalism class. They are really nice and we've been talking about where we're going to college and what we want to major in. Some of them want to major in Journalism, some in English and some don't know yet. I think I've held back from getting to know people in my school because I had all these false impressions about who they are and I've realized that there are kids I like here. Some of us are going to get together to go to the movies this weekend and I've invited Jessie, but she's busy. I'm trying not to be so dependent on her because our lives are moving in different directions. Dr. Fine and I talked about this. I decided that even though Jessie is someone I think will always be a part of my life, it is time for me to branch out and make some new friends because that's what I'm going to need to feel comfortable doing this summer and next year in college. As much as I like them, I can't spend all my time with Marsha and Doug. I'm also feeling more confident about myself, who I am and what I want, and people have noticed a change. I don't feel like the weirdo who went to rehab anymore. I feel like I'm just a high school student like everyone else. It's funny (not funny ha-ha) that all the things I wanted when I started therapy, to be a "normal" kid and have a "normal" family, have started to happen. Except my definition of normal has changed. I, like many other kids, have a single mom who is divorced, but I have a relationship with her and my Dad, and even though he's a gay man who dresses like a woman, he still treats me like a daughter and cares about me and we have a great relationship. When Mom gets too intense for me, which happens about once a week, he listens and helps me chill out by having a good sense of humor and helping me get perspective. Marsha is so funny sometimes! Mom and Marsha have become friends as well, and we've been spending a lot of time in the city with Marsha and Doug. They feel like friends as well as parents. I hope I still like them as much when I live with them. Sometimes I can get sick of people, although that hasn't happened with Jessie yet.

March 23rd, 1988

Spring break is almost here! Mom said I can go to Florida

with Jessie to stay with her grandparents so I am looking forward to that! I love the beach! Third marking period is almost over as well, and the teachers ease up on work for us seniors for the last two months. The senior class trip is coming up; we are going to a matinée of *A Chorus Line*. I'm going with some friends from Journalism class. They've talked me into going to Project Graduation, but not the prom. Been there, done that. Not my thing. But that's OK. A few of my friends kind of feel the same way so we are going to try to plan our own thing for that night. We might go to the mall to hang out in the video game arcade. I've never been really into that but the guys seem to really like it. I do like Pac Man so I guess I will need some rolls of quarters. Now that the weather is getting nicer we're going to start bringing guitars to school and sitting outside during lunch and playing some songs. I've been thinking of writing some again but I can't think of what to write. I kind of like writing for the paper more because I just have to make up questions for the teachers and go from there. Two of the teachers I've interviewed were high school sweethearts and went to Hackettstown High School. Now they're married and teach here. I can't imagine staying here for the rest of my life. There is so much to do and see. They didn't even leave for college; they both went to school in town. It sounds so 1950's to me, but they graduated in '58 so there you go. Life was all about sock hops, and listening to Elvis and Buddy Holly, and bowling. It all sounds so innocent. Especially compared to my Mom's life. She told me that one of the reasons she left home to live on a commune was that she didn't want to turn into Gram and spend her life being a homemaker and taking care of a man. And, she wanted to get away from Gramps. She said that life on the commune was good at first. All the drugs you wanted, no hassles, no establishment. But after a while she realized that it was still a male-dominated society. Somehow, the women ended up doing a majority of the cooking, cleaning and domestic stuff. Once the men finished construction of the buildings they sat around getting high and not doing very much. At first she liked the idea of sexual freedom and being able to sleep with who you wanted with no strings attached. But then she realized that the women were getting the short end of the stick, so to speak, and that many secretly wanted relationships but felt like that would be uncool. There were petty jealousies about who slept with whom and people were getting pregnant, and since relationships were not allowed everybody had to raise everyone's kids. Money was always tight and there was a big fight between the members about what to do. Some just wanted to grow pot and sell it and others wanted an artist collective, and meanwhile people were hungry and the only food was what could be grown or purchased with welfare checks from those who qualified. Mom said that eventually she was longing for regular showers and a steak dinner and a clean bed to sleep in, so she left and got a job. She found that once she gave up drugs and alcohol her thinking was clearer and that she liked the structure of having a job, making her own money, eating what she wanted to eat and taking care of herself. But soon that was not enough, and after attending AA realized that she wanted to re-establish a relationship with me. She felt guilty about leaving and felt like the experiment in communal living was just not what she thought it would be. Except, she hadn't dealt with her issues about my grandfather and men in general, and that's how she ended up in a dysfunctional relationship with Chris. I think she's truly sorry for what happened to me, and is honestly trying to be a better mother. I think she thought she was being a good mother at first, but had no clue about how to parent in this day and age. I guess if all she knew was life with Gram and Gramps and then life on a commune, that didn't prepare her well. Plus, she was only 18 when she had me. A few months older than I am now. I can't imagine being a parent at this point in my life. Maybe someday, but I honestly don't know if I would be a good parent now, either. I think I want to live life for a while and wait until I'm ready to settle down and get married.

Single parenthood is a lot of work. I don't think I want that for myself and I want to at least make a conscious decision to be a parent. I think it's a very important job. It takes a lot of work and sacrifice. Life isn't just about you anymore. Once you have a child, that is a big responsibility. I have forgiven my Mom for her mistakes because I know that she had her own issues and did the best that she could at the time. I've been able to forgive her because she really is trying to do the right thing now. I do feel she genuinely loves me, but she has had to give up a lot of her freedom and I can't help wondering if she resents that. She says no, but I still wonder. I mean, I would resent it. But maybe by the time I'm her age I won't. I have forgiven her but not forgotten. It's taken a lot of work, but she and I are rebuilding trust and have a much better relationship than we did before. It will never be perfect, but I guess no family is. Anyway, what I've learned from this is to think before I act and to really know myself and what I want, so that when I do have kids I can be the parent I want to be.

May 18th, 1988

I am now an adult! I turned 18 yesterday! Now I have to sign consent for things and have to make decisions for myself. It's funny, I don't feel different than I did yesterday, but because of this life has changed. I can vote in the fall for president and therapy is mine and mine only. Mom is still paying because I don't have a job, but I asked her if I can use my savings for it. She said if that's what I want, but that maybe I might want to use it for buying stuff for my dorm room and college. That makes sense, so I told her maybe someday I could pay her back. She told me that she wants to pay because it's her way of making amends. I can understand that. Anyway, last night we went out for dinner to celebrate, with Jessie and a couple of my friends from Journalism class. It was fun, but weird, because it really just felt like another birthday. I don't know what I was expecting, that I would suddenly be this new person because I became an adult? I don't mean that in a bad or sarcastic way, just that it seems so arbitrary. One day I'm 17 the next I'm 18 and have all these rights and privileges. And then this will happen again when I turn 21. That's the big deal to most people because then you can drink legally. What makes someone more mature at 21 than 20? Jessie says I overanalyze things too much. I guess maybe I do. But that is who I am. I don't think she meant it as an insult though. It's just a difference in our personalities. She is more of an "in the moment" person than me. Oh, she got into Oberlin by the way. She wants me to come visit for a weekend in the fall. That sounds like a fun idea if I have the money and can make it happen. I won't have a car because I'll be in the city, but maybe I can take Amtrak. Graduation is in a month! I can't believe it's finally here! Finals are coming up and then the last week of school is just graduation practice. Then Project Graduation and then off to the shore with Mom and Jessie for a week and then I move to NYC! I've been waiting for this for so long and now that it's finally here it feels unreal, like I can't believe it's happening. I told Dr. Fine that. She said that's normal. I'm ready to finish therapy for now. I have mixed feelings. I will miss Dr. Fine but I feel ready to do things on my own. She said I can always come back for a session when I'm on vacation from college or home for a visit. That was nice to hear. It feels weird that soon I won't be living in Hacketts-town anymore. Now, I'll only be home for school vacations and weekends and stuff. So many changes happening. It's scary and exciting all at the same time. But I am ready to start my new life. And I am ready for whatever it brings.

2019

"MOM!!" Cameron yelled. "Grandma is smoking pot!!" Devon, who had been taking care of something in the kitchen when Cameron had burst in, almost caught herself smiling. After all, if that had happened when she was Cameron's age she would have been trying to figure out a way to steal some from Paula. But, she knew this was not the time to share that with Cameron. Instead she turned around from the sink and looked at her younger son.

"Let's talk," she said, taking a seat at the kitchen table and gesturing for Cameron to do the same. "You know that Grandma is very sick and for many people with cancer the only thing that makes them feel better is marijuana. Grandma's doctor prescribed it for her to take away the pain from the cancer and nausea from the chemo."

Cameron nodded as he watched his mother's face. They talked about Paula and her cancer and how it made them both feel sad that she was no longer well. Cameron said he missed having his Grandma at his soccer games and was worried that she was not getting better. Devon hugged him and said, "I wish she was well enough to come to your games. I know she would be there if she could."

Devon began to get teary thinking about that memory as she sat on the floor of the dusty attic of the painted lady Victorian house that had been her home during her high school years. It had begun to show signs of wear, now that her mother had passed after a long battle with cancer. The house was quiet now, with the funeral over and the hospice workers gone. People had paid respects and said the appropriate things. Her children were back at their home in Westchester, with their father, living their lives. She wanted it that way. Devon was, first and foremost a mother, and once the task of readying her mother's house for sale was done, she wanted to be back home with them as well. She had been distracted by attending to all of the details associated with the death of a parent and was just now coming to grips with what had happened. Her mother, Paula, had died. At the age of 68, Paula had initially put up a good fight and had been determined to beat the cancer that eventually killed her. But after three unsuccessful rounds of chemotherapy and radiation, she decided it was time to let nature take its course. Devon, as her only daughter, had tried to be there as much as was possible for someone who had a family of her own and a life of her own in a neighboring state. Devon was close with her mother. After the tumultuous start to their relationship s things slowly improved but really took a more positive turn after she had children. Paula was a devoted grandmother. Devon always wondered how it could be that someone who was clueless as a parent could take to being a grandparent so naturally. From the very beginning Paula was there to help with everything and had developed a close relationship with her grandsons.

Surrounded by old toys that her sons had played with, boxes of mementos, and various pieces of outdated furniture that her mother had refused to part with, Devon looked at the remnants of Paula's life. It was hard to believe she was really gone. Most of the house had been converted to accommodate a sick patient. But the rusty old swing set that her mother had bought years ago for her sons to use during visits still sat unused and forlorn in the back yard. Devon remembered fondly how her boys used to love to play in that yard and how much it was a treat for them to go to Grandma's house. Paula had been there for their soccer games and school award assemblies and never complained about the hours she spent driving to the house in Westchester. She had happily taken an early retirement package at age 52 when Ethan was born in 2003. Cameron followed two years later.

Devon had never intended to be a full time mother. She had graduated from NYU in 1993 with a major in English and took a job for a large publishing company in the city. Starting as an editor's assistant, which was more clerical than she wanted, Devon devoted herself to her career, moving up through the ranks to assistant editor, editor and senior editor. She was on her way to an executive editor title when romance entered her life in an unexpected way. Devon had just broken off a relationship with a guy she had been fairly seriously involved with who worked as a creative director in the Art Department. The relationship had worked because the two of them both had long hours and Devon's apartment was a few short blocks from the office. They were compatible but Devon never felt the chemistry, it was more a bond forged through work.

One night after the break-up she had plans to meet up with her friend Jessie, whom she had known since high school. Jessie also worked in Manhattan and was managing an art gallery in Chelsea. They had reconnected a few years back after both of them were working and living in the city. It had been nice to re-connect with Jessie, since the two of them had gone their separate ways in college. So, when Jessie returned to New York and based herself in the city their friendship was re-kindled and they picked up where they left off. One night, expecting it to be just the two of them as always, Devon walked into the bar and found Jessie already seated at a table with a very handsome, well-dressed man. He looked vaguely familiar, but Devon couldn't place where she'd seen him before. She walked over to the table and Jessie introduced her, saying, "Devon, do you remember my brother Jeff?"

"Wow. He looks even better than he did 16 years ago," Devon thought. Had it really been that long since she had seen him? He was dressed in a well-cut suit and tie and his soft brown hair was neatly styled and combed. "Hi, Devon!" he said, "It's been a long time, but I remember you well!"

Soon the three were lost in conversation and the hours flew by. "So Jeff, you heard all about me during dinner, but the last time I saw you, you were a student at Wesleyan. Tell me what you've been doing."

Jeff smiled, looked at her and said, "I miss those days. They were fun. Well, I graduated from Wesleyan and then went to Columbia for my law degree. After I graduated I clerked for a Supreme Court judge and then got a job at Parker, Wiseman and Lowe; we specialize in Copyright and Entertainment Law. I became a full partner about three years ago so now we're called Parker, Wiseman, Lowe and Goldberg."

Devon found herself lost in Jeff's warm, hazel eyes and easygoing but intelligent, articulate manner. "How is this guy still single?" she wondered. Meanwhile, Jeff was staring into Devon's green eyes, paying rapt attention to her every word. The chemistry was palpable between them. Jessie sat with them, a bemused smile on her face, just watching. She was happily married herself and had, without telling either Jeff or Devon, secretly set up this meeting to play matchmaker. By the end of the evening Jeff was walking Devon home.

"So, Devon," Jeff asked, "are you seeing anyone?"

"Actually, no." Devon replied. "I was seeing a guy who is the creative director in the Art Department at Harper, but we recently broke up. We got along OK and it was a convenient relationship because we worked similar hours and had similar schedules. But there was just no real chemistry. We were more like good friends than boyfriend and girlfriend. How about you?"

"Well," Jeff said, "I'm single too. I was pretty seriously involved with a woman at work, but she wanted marriage and I just wasn't feeling like she was the one, so we parted ways about six months ago."

Little did either of them know that a year later they would be married, and a year after that Devon would give birth to their first son, Ethan. Still sitting in the attic, Devon thought back to the day she introduced Jeff to Paula as her fiancé, and remembered Paula's tears of joy at their wedding.

Devon left her publishing job after having Ethan. Once she became a parent, she realized that was where she wanted to devote her energy. Just seeing this tiny, helpless baby who was totally dependent on her released a maternal instinct she didn't realize she had. In two years Devon had gone from having a family that consisted of Paula and her father (who was now officially a woman after having a sex-change operation) and Doug, her father Marsha's partner, to include Jeff, Jessie, Jessie's parents and now a son. And all of them wanted to be involved in her life, in a good way. Ethan was coming into the world with a tight-knit group of loving adults who doted on him ceaselessly. And then with the addition of Cameron they were just as excited.

Devon found adjusting to motherhood much easier and more natural than she had anticipated. Jeff, although he worked long hours, was an attentive father and close with his sons. He tried to limit the number of work-related extra-curricular social events he attended. Jeff was more of an introvert like Devon and never really enjoyed the nights of steaks and scotch and cigars that were popular among his colleagues. While he didn't totally abstain from alcohol, Devon preferred not to have it in the house and he was fine with that.

Jeff and Devon bought a nice house in Bedford Hills, which had an excellent school district and lots of community activities for children. Devon developed a network of friends that she met through her kids – other mothers who had had professional lives and were now either working at home, working part-time or volunteering. She had a book club that she attended weekly, which kept her intellectually stimulated and in the loop about what was being published. And she was thinking about writing her own first novel. Devon's life was full and satisfying.

And then Paula got sick. For two years Devon commuted back and forth to Hackettstown to help with her mother's care. She made sure that the boys could maintain a relationship with their grandmother even though she was ill, and at times that was a challenge, because while they loved their grandmother, they wanted to be with their friends and at home where the action was. And it seemed like their sports were more and more time-consuming. Once Paula became housebound Devon had to find ways to make the boys comfortable at the house in Hackettstown, because seeing them brought Paula so much joy.

As she sat on the floor and memories of her life flooded through her, her eyes spied a box. It was labeled "Devon." Unable to resist she opened it. Inside was her favorite teddy bear, which she had saved from her days living with her grandparents, her high school and college diplomas, her high school report cards, and most importantly, her diary. Emotion overtook Devon as she picked it up. She felt tears starting. Did she really want to relive those years? But, at the same time, she felt compelled to read it. She took a deep breath and opened the cover.

Devon read it in one sitting. There was no clock in the attic and her phone was downstairs so she had no idea how long it took or what time it was. As the pages flew past, she realized that what she had penned so many years before was a story of hurt, upheaval and trauma that worked itself through and ended better than she could have hoped. Despite the losses and pain, Devon ended up with a larger, more loving family than she could have ever imagined. She would mourn Paula and there would always be a hole in her heart, a piece missing now that her mother was gone, but Devon was grateful that through it all, she and her mother had developed a wonderful bond and that she was able to be there for her at the end. And her mother's love would live on through the bonds of her family.

Devon took a deep breath, let it out and said aloud, "Thank you for everything, Paula, Sunflower…Mom." As she closed the door to the attic and headed down the stairs, her mind turned to her children – Ethan's PSATs next week, Cameron's last soccer tournament before camp – and Jeff's loving arms waiting for her at home.

ABOUT THE AUTHOR

Amy Price lives in Eldorado, a subdivision of Santa Fe, New Mexico. This is her second novel. Amy has a deep passion for music and she currently focuses on hosting three different music radio shows, all of which she self-produces and programs. They air on 96.9 KMRD-LP (which streams live at KMRD.fm/listen), HomeGrownRadioNJ.com and WNTI.org Amy also writes a non-fiction blog about self-development called amypriceblog.com. In her past professional life she was a NJ Licensed Psychologist and School Psychologist who practiced in both clinical and mostly school settings. She shares her life and love for New Mexico with her loving husband Jody and their two cats.